TRUE VOL. 2

52 STORIES ABOUT GOD SHOWING UP IN THE EVERY DAY

IRENE DUNLAP

"Now many will hear of the glorious things he did for me, and stand in awe before the Lord, and put their trust in him."

—Psalm 40:3, LB

TRUE VOL. 2

52 STORIES ABOUT GOD SHOWING UP IN THE EVERY DAY

IRENE DUNLAP

ZONDERVAN®

ZONDERVAN.com/
AUTHORTRACKER
follow your favorite authors

Youth Specialties.com

True, Vol. 2: 52 Stories About God Showing Up in the Every Day
Copyright © 2007 by Irene Dunlap

Youth Specialties products, 300 S. Pierce St., El Cajon, CA 92020 are published by Zondervan, 5300 Patterson Ave. SE, Grand Rapids, MI 49530.

ISBN-10: 0-310-25302-0
ISBN-13: 978-0-310-25302-0

Web site addresses listed in this book were current at the time of publication. Please contact Youth Specialties via e-mail (YS@YouthSpecialties.com) to report URLs that are no longer operational and replacement URLs if available.

Creative Team: Dave Urbanski, Kristi Robison, SharpSeven Design, Rich Cairnes, and Janie Wilkerson
Cover Design by SharpSeven Design

Printed in the United States of America

07 08 09 10 11 12 • 21 20 19 18 17 16 15 14 13 12 11 10 9 8 7 6 5 4 3 2 1

CONTENTS

9   **DEDICATION**

11   **ACKNOWLEDGMENTS**

15   **INTRODUCTION**

21   **CHAPTER ONE: HE IS A GOD OF DELIVERANCE.**

23   **Out of the Churning Waters**...Robert Dallas Mehl, as told to Loretta Miller Mehl
27   **Second Chance**...Aisha K. Moore, Esq.
32   **The Brake of a Lifetime**...Bruce Salvati
36   **In His Hands**...Phillip LaRue
40   **A Journey of Love**...Linda Flock
44   **Near the Edge**...Sirena Van Schaik

49   **CHAPTER TWO: HE IS A GOD OF INFINITE SUPPORT.**

51   **The Plain Fact**...Jackie Abruzzini
56   **The New Girl**...Tiffany O'Neill
61   **Thank You, Fozzie**...Rusty Fischer
67   **Stranded**...Jenna King
72   **Carried by the Good Shepherd**...Katherine Knickerbocker
77   **A Flicker of Hope**...Rachel Giffin
81   **Time and Again**...Anonymous

87   **CHAPTER THREE: HE IS A GOD OF TRANSFORMATION.**

89   **Different**...Ace Armstrong
95   **Back on the Right Track**...Kristin Greene
99   **Opening to Love**...Ashley Kinden
103   **Never Alone**...Laura Farrar
108   **Running Toward My Fears**...Anonymous
117   **The Crash**...Pamela Reilly

123 **CHAPTER FOUR: HE IS A GOD OF RECOVERY AND RESTORATION.**

125   **Reclaimed**...Eric Hixon
137   **Satisfied**...Paul Mishoe
145   **Mesmerized**...Brittany Cantrell
151   **My Continuous Battle**...Sarah Packard
156   **Stitches, Scars, and Survival**...Sarah Porter
161   **All the Broken Pieces**...Louise Russell
166   **Piece by Piece**...Katie Skarvinko

171 **CHAPTER FIVE: HE IS A GOD OF CONSTANT COMPANIONSHIP.**

173   **The Voice Inside**...Rachel Giffin
177   **Sinking Sand**...Nancy C. Anderson
180   **Closer to the Fire**...Madeline Shomos
185   **Sufficient for Me**...Amanda Reese
188   **Living Fortress**...Brandon Tamblin
194   **Swimming the Walk**...Samuel R. Stephens
199   **Amazing Love**...Laurie Vines

205 **CHAPTER SIX: HE IS A GOD OF ANSWERS AND GUIDANCE.**

207   **Pointless Prayer**...J. M. Butler
212   **The Prom Date**...Diana L. James
216   **In the Current**...Josh Nordgren
222   **Redirected**...Nicole Pipke
230   **Clearing the Way**...Haley Vile
236   **A Snapshot Divinely Composed**...Kellyn Walker

241 **CHAPTER SEVEN: HE IS A GOD OF REFUGE AND COMFORT.**

243 **Hope in the Mourning**...Alie Aukerman
247 **Love That Heals**...Elsa Kok Colopy
251 **Letting Go**...Kristina Marie Drummond
254 **Look How They Shine**...Marleigh Dunlap
261 **Minute by Minute**...Ryan Fischer
265 **Enduring the Unendurable**...Kristen McNulty
270 **On the Trail**...Tom Beigle

277 **CHAPTER EIGHT: HE IS A GOD WITH A POWERFUL PRESENCE.**

279 **Still Connected**...Susan Rae Burns
283 **Streams of Mercy**...Joseph Laughon
288 **God Comes to History**...Casey Day
292 **Playing by the Rules**...Sandra Holmes McGarrity
297 **The Richer Ones**...Jessica Dunagan
301 **What a Ride**...Alistair Merryman

309 **AFTERWORD**

311 **GOT A GREAT GOD STORY?**

313 **GIVING BACK**

315 **IRENE DUNLAP**

317 **PERMISSIONS AND BIOGRAPHIES**

DEDICATION

To my mother, Angela Jack, who has been a blessing and an inspiration of faith throughout my life. Thank you for teaching me how to trust God. I've learned to "put it in his hands" by watching you do it over and over again. Your constant love and your prayers in support of my work have meant the world to me.

Love you forever and ever.

ACKNOWLEDGMENTS

As with *True Vol. 1*, I thank God for his faithfulness, perfect timing, direction, and grace at every turn as I worked on this project. It's my deepest hope these stories will honor and glorify God's works and name beyond my highest imagination.

Thanks again to Gina Romanello for your incredible skills and willingness to help me with whatever I needed to make this book come together. You're a pro and a great friend. And thanks to Noelle Champagne for your creative efforts in helping with the call for stories.

Thanks to my husband, Kent, and my kids Marleigh and Weston; to my mother, Angela Jack; my in-laws Hank and Bonnie Dunlap; and to my sisters Kathi Fischer, Pattie Buford, Pamela Brown, Jeffra Lokteff, Greta Dunlap, and Lisa Vitello, and their families for your constant love and support.

To Juan Casas for connecting me with Youth Specialties and for your belief in this project and in me.

To Laine Latimer for your heart for this series and your willingness to help spread the word about it through your generous contribution in the area of publicity.

To Jennifer Briner for graciously helping sweeten the final manuscript. Thanks for leveraging your knowledge of Scripture and lending your eagle eye to help me polish up typos and smooth out some of the rough edges. You're awesome.

Thanks to some of my faithful friends who supported and encouraged me through this process: Patty Hansen, Stacey and Rocky Robbins, Deborah Calvert, Marcia Kirschbaum, Jill Shannon, Christine Vile, Eric Briner, and Erik and Leslie Williams.

To those who donated their time and opinions by reading every story considered for this book—you played an extremely important part in the selection of stories, and I thank each of you for your dedication and insight: Brooke McKinley, Michelle Lewis, Melissa Oldreive, Sierra Chavez, Whitney Freeman, Amanda Severns, Evelyn Hall, Alicia Sparks, Nadia Ramnarain, Vicki Ribar, Gerald Moore, Katie Goodwin, Sanyuja Zambare, Lydia Irby, and Jordan Carr.

Finally, to everyone on the publishing team at Youth Specialties and Zondervan: Jay Howver, Mark Oestreicher, Roni Meek, David Conn, Holly Sharp, and Renee Altson. Thanks for your dedication to making this an excellent, successful book. Thanks to editors Dave Urbanski and Kristi Robison for your excellent work in refining the manuscript and to Janie Wilkerson and Rich Cairnes for your awesome proofreading skills. And to the marketing team, David Welch, Jamie Hinojosa, Leslie Speyers, and Leslie Lutes—thank you for leveraging your collective creative skills to help bring attention to this title.

It's because of everyone mentioned above that this book will have the potential to help readers gain a bet-

ter understanding of God's character. Again my gratitude goes to each one of you for the special role you played in the development of this book.

Bless you all!

INTRODUCTION

What humans seem to know about God comes from many sources. Some experience him through visions; some hear him speak into their hearts; some have a feeling he's guiding and directing them. Various accounts and descriptions of God have been given over thousands of years.

But if the God of the universe has anything to say about himself, I think we should take note. The word *God* describes a power higher than human beings—a supernatural and Supreme Being. With that in mind, examining what God knows to be true about his own character might be a good start.

Here's just *some* of what God has to say about himself:

- "I am the light of the world. Whoever follows me will never walk in darkness, but will have the light of life." (John 8:12)

- "I am compassionate." (Exodus 22:27)

- "I am the Lord, who heals you." (Exodus 15:26)

- "I will strengthen you." (Isaiah 45:5)

- "I am the Lord your God, who teaches you what is best for you, who directs you in the way you should go." (Isaiah 48:17)

- "'For I know the plans I have for you,' declares the Lord, 'plans to prosper you and not to harm you, plans to give you hope and a future.'" (Jeremiah 29:11)

- "'I am merciful,' declares the Lord." (Jeremiah 3:12)

- "I will be with you; I will never leave you nor forsake you." (Joshua 1:5)

And if for some reason we don't believe God is accessible, he tells us this: "When you come looking for me, you'll find me. Yes, when you get serious about finding me and want it more than anything else, I'll make sure you won't be disappointed" (Jeremiah 29:13, *The Message*).

And finally—"I am the Lord, the God of all mankind. Is anything too hard for me?" (Jeremiah 32:27)

What God says about himself is validated by the way he stands behind his Word. God's Word, after all, lives through the way he makes himself known to us when we choose to be in relationship with him: "For the word of God is living and active" (Hebrews 4:12).

Jesus describes God's Word in his teachings: "The words I say to you are not just my own. Rather, it is the Father, living in me, who is doing his work" (John 14:10).

If you're still wondering just who this God guy is, perhaps you can catch a glimpse of him through these modern-day experiences of how others detect God's presence and relate to him as the Friend and Father he desires to be.

Those who've chosen to tell their stories in this book bring with them authenticity reflecting the Scripture: "In this new life, one's race or nationality or social position is not important; such things mean nothing. Whether a person has Christ is what matters, and he is equally available to all" (Colossians 3:11).

To the contributors I dedicate this verse: "I am thankful to God all the time for you. I am thankful for the loving-favor God has given to you because you belong to Christ Jesus. He has made your lives rich in every way. Now you have power to speak for him. He gave you good understanding" (1 Corinthians 1:4-5).

It's my privilege to share these true experiences and respond to God's directives to tell others about him:

- "Make the most of your chances to tell others the Good News." (Colossians 4:5)

- "But my life is worth nothing unless I use it for doing the work assigned me by the Lord Jesus—the work of telling others the Good News about God's wonderful kindness and love." (Acts 20:24, NLT)

I pray the experiences shared in the coming pages help you better understand the Creator of the universe and prompt you to want to find his heart, hold it in yours, and never let it go.

Irene Dunlap

"I am not praying for these alone, but also for the future believers who will come to me because of the testimony of these."

—John 17:20

HE IS A GOD OF DELIVERANCE.

"Do not be afraid. Stand firm and you will see the deliverance the Lord will bring you today."
—Exodus 14:13

OUT OF THE CHURNING WATERS

"We felt we were doomed to die and saw how powerless we were to help ourselves; but that was good, for then we put everything into the hands of God, who alone could save us, for he can even raise the dead."

—2 Corinthians 1:9-10, LB

When summer approached, my parents prepared for their yearly vacation to visit friends and relatives in far-off states. I'd gone with them numerous times across the scorching desert, following the never-ending white lines stretching for miles of highway. Now as a teenager I wanted the freedom to spend time with my friends, practice guitar, hike in the mountains, and swim in our pool. I finally persuaded my parents to leave me at home, convincing them I'd be perfectly safe while they were away.

The day dawned beautiful and warm in Southern California. With Mom and Dad gone I felt I could do whatever I liked. Having the house all to myself sounded good, but then my friend Ross called and asked if I wanted to go snorkeling at Newport Beach. He'd called to check on the surf conditions and found the day would be mild with a low undertow and clear visibility—perfect for snorkeling.

I did not have snorkeling equipment, so I borrowed some fins and a wet suit. The booties were missing, so I substituted tennis shoes. I tied the laces tightly on both sides around the fins' steel buckles.

Since daylight hours were much longer in the summer, we weren't too concerned about starting out late. By the time we arrived, it was still nice out, and the sandy beach looked beautiful with rhythmic waves splashing against the shoreline.

Ross and I swam out a good distance and dove, checking out the fish among the seaweed. We planned to dive down and look at shafts of sunlight that caused spectacular displays of fluorescent blue, green, and orange.

Ross stopped to break open a sea urchin so he could feed the fish surrounding us when he noticed the water becoming turbulent and murky. While surfacing a few moments later, he told me the conditions looked risky and we should make our way back to shore. Since the riptide was increasing, Ross suggested getting out of the water where large rocks provided a calm break in the surf.

I followed him with my snorkel up and face in the water. We progressed slowly, fighting the choppy current.

Finally, I felt my fins hitting the bottom and tried to stand up. But when I looked forward, I saw we were surrounded by a tunnel of water reaching up over our heads. The water had been drawn up between two rows of rocks that extended about a hundred yards into the ocean, spread about 15 feet apart. We'd been swimming in the middle of it!

Before I could react, what seemed like tons of water came crashing down on me.

Okay, God, here we go, I thought, as I spun around underwater holding my head, trying to protect myself. I then cried out, "God, *please* help us get out of this!" as the water tossed me from side to side in what appeared to be an impossible situation to escape.

The next thing I remember was rolling onto my side on top of a giant rock. I got to my feet and realized I'd been thrown completely out of the water and was now standing on a high cliff about 15 feet above the surf. Seconds before, I'd frantically tried to escape the churning mass and the danger of being crushed to death.

As I struggled to survive, God had swept me up and placed me in a safe place, high upon a rock. I gazed at the hazardous turbulence below and searched for Ross. "Oh, God," I prayed, "please save Ross, too!"

Moments later I shouted with relief when my friend ran toward me. He, too, had been thrown clear of danger. I gave him a bear hug as I joyfully pounded his back.

When I stooped down to evaluate my condition, I realized my feet hurt—the fins were gone, the steel buckles still dangling from the tennis shoe laces. The powerful waves had ripped the fins from my feet. My knee was bleeding from an abrasion underneath a four-inch cut in my wet suit. Otherwise I felt fine—no injuries a bandage couldn't handle. But when my sister Sheri saw me, she exclaimed, "Your bruises are huge!"

Several weeks later Mom questioned me: "Did anything dangerous happen while we were away?" Usually, I would've tried to evade or deny an answer. I didn't want her to think I couldn't handle my own life, but she had a different tone in her voice. When I confessed what had happened that day, she shared her amazing experience of how God had awakened her from sleep to pray for me. I confirmed it was no coincidence.

Mom said she and Dad had arrived in Pennsylvania on the day of our snorkeling scare. She retired early, weary from the trip, but an overwhelming urge to pray for me awakened her. Not knowing why I needed prayer, she asked for my protection and that whatever the circumstances God would be near and keep me safe. She told me she realized she could do nothing to protect me, and she placed me in God's hands.

In the aftermath of that terrifying event my friend and I stood in awe, watching the waves break far below the top of the cliff where we stood. We agreed God had rescued us; we could've been killed, hurled against those boulders. Without God's intervention neither of us could explain what had happened. We watched for a long time, astonished that the waves never once came anywhere near as high as the rock where we landed.

I often paraphrase David in Psalm 40:2 when I look back on that day: God pulled me out of the churning waters and placed me safely upon a rock.

Robert Dallas Mehl, as told to Loretta Miller Mehl

SECOND CHANCE

"Yet the Lord longs to be gracious to you; he rises to show you compassion."

—Isaiah 30:18

My mother paced up and down the hallway. She was making me nervous, as usual.

"All right, what's the plan again?"

I sighed, responding in a casual but slightly annoyed tone. I wanted her to believe the lie.

"I'm meeting Tara at the movies in Webster. We're going to grab some food. I'm coming straight home."

She hesitated, sensing something was wrong.

When I was younger, I prayed often. I could always feel God near me, guiding my path. I was tuned into him.

Now it was more important to be popular and have a boyfriend. None of the guys I liked were Christians, not by a long shot. So I turned a deaf ear to the stirring in my heart, the nudging at my conscience. Soon I could

lie without even feeling guilty. I'd mastered the art of deception.

"I give up," she said simply, throwing up her hands in exasperation. "Be home before midnight."

Yes!

I jumped into my tiny car and backed out of the driveway before she could change her mind. I glanced down at my watch. It was 8:30 p.m. Plenty of time.

I was going to Robert's house. His parents were gone for the weekend. Tara would cover for me; she was leaving her house and attending the movies with friends, just in case my mother called her parents to verify.

But my plan was to be alone with Robert for the next three hours. For the first time in months I felt a very small nagging at the corner of my mind. *Maybe I shouldn't go.*

No, I argued internally, *I love Robert. I want this.*

Then I thought, *What about my vow of virginity?* I shook my head. I wasn't going to deal with that right now. The opportunity had presented itself, and I was going with it.

I pressed my foot on the accelerator, pushing my car past the speed limit. My conscience was getting the best of me, and I had to silence it.

Suddenly, a barrage of warnings flooded me: *Slow down. Go to Tara's house. Don't do this. Slow down!*

I was almost to Robert's—just a few more streets to go. I only had to get through one major intersection. As I approached it, the light changed to yellow.

I can make it, I thought, pushing down on the gas. A brown Mustang was waiting on the opposite side of the intersection, signaling a left turn.

I can make it!

I floored it. The Mustang jerked forward. He was going for it, too.

"No! I have the right of way!" I screamed.

I slammed on the brakes, but I was going too fast, and my little car couldn't handle the sudden resistance. I heard screeching and felt my car skidding. In that instant I was overwhelmed by thoughts, sights, and sounds. The Mustang was going to hit me—or the other way around. I also noticed I hadn't fastened my seat belt.

The impact was deafening. I felt my neck snap as my body lifted out of the seat. Some part deep within knew I was going to die after I hit the windshield.

Time seemed to stand still while I soared through the air. I envisioned my mother's face. I thought about my grandparents. I hadn't visited them in months. *What about my father?* I'd refused to see him.

Mommy, Daddy, please forgive me, I silently pleaded.

I didn't want to die.

"OH GOD, HELP ME!" I yelled the most primal and sincere plea I'd ever uttered. Then everything went black.

I don't know how long I was unconscious. When I opened my eyes, I noticed the driver of the Mustang sitting in the middle of the intersection. People had left their cars and were talking to him, standing a few feet from

me. No one had come to look inside my tiny car. I think they were certain I was dead.

I tried sitting up, but my entire body ached. Slowly, I opened the door of my car. As I shifted my legs, a sharp pain shot through my right ankle into my foot. I eased out of the car and made my way to the curb where I quickly sat back down. I noticed the bystanders staring at me as if seeing a ghost.

I watched as police cars arrived on the scene, driving on the sidewalk to navigate past traffic. Staring down the street, I could see traffic backed up for miles.

I focused on the black asphalt. I couldn't remember what happened. My mind was a jumble of images. Two people approached, speaking in soft tones. It took a minute before I realized they were Robert's parents. They'd been stuck in traffic, and when they saw my car, they panicked and pulled over. I'm sure they guessed where I was headed, but they didn't say anything.

Before long Robert showed up. He'd heard the collision from his house and come to investigate.

Finally, my mother and her husband arrived. She became frantic as she saw the shattered glass and demolished car frames, then she thanked God over and over again when she caught sight of me alive. Her reaction brought me some relief. Of course she must've figured out I'd lied about where I was going. *Sorry* seemed too small a word for everything I'd done.

The officers on the scene advised my parents to have me checked out even though I insisted I was fine and had refused an ambulance. At the hospital the doctor in the emergency room asked me to describe the accident. I told him about the head-on collision and admitted I hadn't worn a seat belt. I also described the make and model of my car.

He looked up suddenly and lowered his clipboard.

"How did you manage to stay in the car?" he asked.

I shrugged my shoulders. "I don't know," I responded. "Maybe I hit the steering wheel. I felt like I was airborne, and then everything went black."

He examined my head closely, studied the X-rays and then scribbled notes on his pad. He called my mother into the room and sat back on the small stool.

"My best guess is you didn't hit the steering wheel, since you don't have any head trauma or obvious bruising such an impact would cause. There's no telling what kept you from going through that windshield. Interestingly, I also have no valid explanation as to why your right ankle and foot are bothering you."

But I knew. I'd used that ankle and foot to press on the gas pedal to see Robert that night. But God had intervened through his amazing grace, power, and compassion. He'd given me a second chance at life—a second chance to get back on the right path. I sat there feeling totally unworthy but incredibly thankful.

As I slowly recovered, I realized the pain in my ankle was a very small price to pay for the mistakes I'd made. And that pain was also a huge reminder of how much worse things could've turned out.

Aisha K. Moore, Esq.

THE BRAKE OF A LIFETIME

> *"But that is why God had mercy on me, so that Christ Jesus could use me as a prime example of his great patience with even the worst sinners. Then others will realize that they, too, can believe in him and receive eternal life."*
>
> —1 Timothy 1:16, NLT

When I was in high school, I started having what seemed like anxiety attacks—scary situations where it became really hard for me to breathe. It got worse, so my parents took me to a specialist to find out what was going on. I endured a ton of awful tests, including having a bunch of needles stuck in my skin, until the doctor finally diagnosed me with a severe case of asthma.

To treat the symptoms I had to get adrenaline shots twice a week. So I went from not being able to breathe to being completely hopped up all the time. I often couldn't sleep because of the medication, and I'd stay up until two or three in the morning practicing guitar.

One of my other obsessions was fixing up my car. I painted it black and then jacked it up in the back with big giant tires and huge air shocks. It was so high in the back I couldn't see much without relying on the side mirrors.

The artificial intensity I experienced from the adrenaline mixed with my rebellious and moody nature and played out through the way I drove. My usual exit from the house was to jump in my car, slam it into reverse, peel out, and speed away. Often I drove around the neighborhood looking for guys willing to race me. As a result I'd received a couple of speeding tickets over several months.

Instead of realizing I deserved what I got and needed to change my habits, I felt picked on and angry about the tickets. So I just let them pile up and ignored them. Of course, they eventually went to warrant, and I was called into court. The fines had built up to the point I was either going to have to make payments for what seemed like the rest of my life or see if the judge would give me community service and reduce the amount to something I could actually afford at age 17.

On the morning I was to appear before the judge, I grabbed the pile of tickets and headed out to my car. I was of course still hopped up on adrenaline but also seriously irritated with the situation. I was thinking about how I was going to peel out and take out some of my aggression.

I climbed in and slammed the door. I put my foot on the brake while turning the key and then jammed into reverse to peel out. That's when the weirdest, strangest thing happened.

When I went to lift my foot from the brake to switch over to the gas pedal, my foot wouldn't respond to what my brain was telling it to do. I couldn't move my foot. It just stuck there as if held down by some sort of powerful glue. Frustrated, I started swearing, put the car back in neutral, and began pulling at my leg. I was so confused I couldn't make any sense of what was happening. The whole thing seemed surreal.

Then suddenly, my foot came up off the pedal as if nothing had happened. Instead of trying to sit there and analyze what'd happened, I was now more irritated than when I first got into the car. Finally back in control, I went to move my foot to the accelerator, and as I was doing so, I looked in my side mirror to check for anything behind me. My fist was gripping the gear knob. Just as I was about to jam it into reverse, I noticed three little girls step out from behind my car. Instantly, I realized if I'd peeled out in reverse, I would've plowed into them.

I lost it right there and then. Knowing I'd come so close to taking all three of their lives hit me hard. And the realization that my bad attitude and reckless rage could've ruined so much—their lives, my life, and the lives of all of our loved ones—finally stopped me in my tracks.

I made my way to the courthouse with a more humble attitude and a new approach to driving. Soon after, I began to calm down and generally take things a bit slower. I also began regularly going to church. Before long I got baptized, and I remember feeling like a totally new person.

That one experience changed the course of my life. I put my anger and rage long behind me and put all those late-night hours of guitar playing to good use as a worship leader.

I often think about how different my life would've been if my foot had hit the gas when I wanted it to. I totally believe it was only because of God's grace and a couple of buff guardian angels who momentarily held my foot on the brake that those three girls are alive and I am where I am today.

I also believe if things had turned out otherwise, I would've been on the road to a failed life. But I don't think God was willing to accept that for me. Instead he chose to give me the "brake" of a lifetime.

Bruce Salvati

IN HIS HANDS

> *"For who is God besides the Lord? And who is the Rock except our God? It is God who arms me with strength and makes my way perfect."*
>
> —Psalm 18:31-32

Venezuela.

I've always wanted to travel and have a chance to serve people in need, so the opportunity appealed to me when my sister Natalie and I were asked to go to Venezuela with a group on a mission trip. Interestingly, the tattoo on my back that reads "Slave to Christ" in ancient Hebrew got us the invitation. I was slated to do this huge talk on the subject of being a Christian and how tattoos could be a positive way to show faith. That became the theme of the trip. Bracelets of a photocopy of my tattoo were even made for all the teens on the mission.

In addition to speaking and playing music, I was asked to be part of an overnight campout and mini-retreat into the jungle with a small group of guys. To prevent us from contracting malaria, we needed to take a prescription drug.

Everything came together, and we began the journey, stopping first in Florida a few days early to meet with some of the leaders and better prepare for the trip. I'd begun the course of anti-malaria medication, taking the first in a series of pills. That one pill began my own version of *Mission: Impossible.*

What we didn't know then but found out later is a small percentage of people who take this particular anti-malaria drug have a seriously bad reaction to it. I quickly became delusional and couldn't think straight. I was really paranoid when anyone looked at me and even thought people were following me. The worst was that a *Real World*-type show wanted to feature Natalie and me, and I was so out of it, it wasn't funny. I'm sure the TV production crew wondered what was up with me. I was totally sleep-deprived—I'd been too paranoid to sleep, thinking someone was trying to kill me. All my worst fears seemed real. My mind was so freaked out I began having delusions someone was breaking into my parents' house. I barely ate, thinking people had poisoned the food.

Although all of this was going on, I stuck it out and got on the plane to Caracas, Venezuela. There were about 350 people in the group; unfortunately, my mom and sister weren't even near me. A few days into the trip, for no particular reason I walked out the front entrance of our hotel and began wandering the streets alone, quickly becoming disoriented and ultimately lost. The city was really eerie, making my state of paranoia even worse. As I wandered down a street in an older section of town, a group of people began chasing me. I'll never know if they were legitimately planning to jump me or what, but my dark, weird mindset intensified the whole experience.

Somehow I got away from them and remained lost in Caracas for hours, going through the streets, not knowing what was happening, and trying to find the hotel. I ended up in an area the police had barricaded. All at once

people started screaming at me in Spanish. Then several police cars pulled up, and the officers got out and surrounded me with their guns drawn. They pulled me down to the ground, handcuffed me, and then took me to the American Embassy. It took some translating and a few phone calls until they finally figured out what I was doing there and where I was staying.

Meanwhile, our group at the hotel had realized I was missing. They found my mom, who then called my dad back home to tell him I was lost and asked him to pray. Luckily, knowing me as well as he does, he began to suspect the drug could've had something to do with my strange behavior. He made some phone calls and did some research. Before long he was in contact with two different people who'd had this same kind of reaction. He got pretty scared when one of the guys confided he'd wanted to kill himself but luckily couldn't find a gun.

Well, needless to say, my keynote speaker duties were over and so was my participation in the mission. They put me on a plane flying home where my dad was waiting. I must've looked like someone else walking off that plane since I'd lost 27 pounds. I'd slept a grand total of nine hours over the course of the week and was totally dehydrated. I couldn't feel whether I was hungry or even in pain. I was so weak I couldn't walk, so they put me in a wheelchair to get me out of the airport.

It took weeks for me to recover from the side effects of the drug. For the longest time my mom's eyes would change colors when she was talking to me. It was so crazy how this thing smaller than an aspirin could have complete control over me and change everything in my personality. I think I'd rather have had malaria than have gone through that long, twisted nightmare.

Worst of all was that in my altered state of mind, I hurt a lot of people by saying and doing things I wouldn't

normally have said or done. Everyone was pretty tripped out and not sure what to make of the way I was behaving. I was humbled as never before—there I was, a recording artist and the chosen keynote speaker, and everyone was looking at me like I was a total whack.

It took a long time for my feeling of fear to go away, and I had to deal with a ton of emotions. I questioned God with the usual, "Why me? Why on a mission trip, wanting to serve people? Why did I have to end up making a fool of myself, and now what did people think of this Phillip LaRue guy who'd had all this success?"

Then about a month after the trip the reason for this insane experience hit me. I came to realize the celebrity I have doesn't make me any more resilient to the world or able to control my life more than anyone else. I'm still vulnerable and very much human.

And I realized more than ever how good God is and how he's undeniably in control of my destiny. Given my state of mind during that trip, I could've ended up missing for much longer—or worse. The scenarios are endless. Yet when I lost complete control, God protected me and showed me my life truly is in his hands.

Phillip LaRue

A JOURNEY OF LOVE

"From the Lord comes deliverance."

—Psalm 3:8

He and I were very close. I was Daddy's little girl in every way. I saw him as my protector. And then one month before my high school graduation, my dad died.

I was angry at God. He'd taken away the one person who loved me. I never questioned my dad's love, and I always felt it.

On the other hand, I didn't feel my mother's love, and I didn't trust her. We didn't have a close relationship for many different reasons. However, deep inside I needed her but wouldn't let her know, and I wouldn't show her any emotion whatsoever. We continued on a road of disagreement, anger, frustration, and pain after Dad was gone.

Years later I realized I had to find a way to allow my mother in my life no matter how difficult it was going to be. She was getting older, and I didn't want any regrets. I began to accept her into my life and heart. At last I found the ability to forgive her for all of the bad things she'd said and done to me, but I never told her I'd forgiven her.

We had two years of a closer relationship after that; still, I never felt her love the way I needed and wanted to.

Then one morning I called her and didn't get an answer. About 30 minutes later my brother called to tell me my mother had unexpectedly died. It didn't immediately register. I just sat there in silence. Then it was as if someone stuck a knife in my heart. The pain was so deep; I was consumed with such strong emotion I was frightened.

I immediately began praying—really more like pleading with God. Over and over again I kept imploring, "I can't! I can't do this! I can't go on. I can't survive this. I can't believe this!"

My mother and I were just finding a balance in our relationship. How could God do this to me? It wasn't fair. I needed her love and I needed her. I'd spent my life wanting her to love me, and now it was too late.

The funeral was so difficult; I didn't think I would make it through. During the services at church I sobbed uncontrollably. I stared at the cross hanging on the wall behind the altar. Silently, I prayed for God to help me. I prayed in ways I never had before. I've never felt so much pain in my life—not even after losing my dad, who I'd loved more than anyone. I wondered to myself, *Can I die from this much pain?* I honestly wasn't sure.

When the funeral was over and I came back home, I didn't know what to do with my pain. Then the idea of writing a letter to my mother came to me. At first it seemed like a strange thing to do, but I knew I had to find some way to express emotion to her. Even though she was physically gone, I could only hope that if I let the words out of my soul and admitted I'd always loved Mom and needed her, she'd somehow know.

So I wrote and wrote, telling her she was a good mother and I was going to miss her. Then painful stuff began to come out. I knew I had to get it all off my chest, so I told her all my life I thought she didn't love me and about how I'd lashed out at her a lot because of how much that had hurt me. When I was done with the letter, I set it by a photograph of Mom and read it aloud.

It was an extremely emotional moment and—I now believe—the beginning of healing. It was God's response to my prayers to help me through my pain. That letter began what I refer to as a miracle.

Soon I began writing poems, which came out more like conversations with my mother. At times the words sounded like answers from her. They just flowed as if I were recopying them. The most amazing thing is that along the way, I felt my mother's love. I also felt as if she and I took an extraordinary journey together through my writing, and she was with me the whole way. How was it possible? I had no idea except to think God had somehow divinely intervened.

Then one night I had a dream about my mother— only I think it was more like a visit. In this dream we were out to lunch together, and she looked so young, so full of life. When our lunches were served, Mom took some salad from her plate and put it on mine, as if she'd given me a gift. After I ate the salad, I leaned over the table and looked into my mother's eyes. I put my hand on hers and asked, "How old are you?" She replied, "I am one." Did she mean "one with God"? I had so many questions for her, but before I could say anything, she looked at me and said, "Forgiveness is what you gave me in the end."

I woke up crying and realized somewhere deep inside me that Mom knew I'd forgiven her, even though I'd never told her.

She knew.

But how?

I had other dreams soon after. In one of them I asked my mom what it's like when you die, and she replied, "Just like they say it is." I felt a strong sense of comfort from that dream.

After that dream I knelt down and spoke to God again. I thanked him for what he'd done for me. Somehow, through a miracle—because it would have to be one—God brought me my mother's love. I had no other explanation for the certainty I felt about that.

People say something good often comes from something bad, and God moves in mysterious ways. He always has a plan. We just don't always have faith.

My faith was strengthened when God delivered me from my pain and the void I'd felt all my life. The most important thing for me, which is so significant to my well-being and my survival, is to know my mother loved me.

Now I know.

Linda Flock

NEAR THE EDGE

"I hate you," I whispered to the empty room, but I knew he was listening.

I've never doubted the presence of God or that he in his infinite wisdom has a plan for the human race. What I did doubt was God's plan for me, and who I hated was God.

Every night tears sprang to my eyes, and I listened to the footsteps of my stepfather as he stumbled into my bedroom and clumsily raped me. The pain I felt from being at his mercy left me numb and sick all at once. Every night as I lay with my head on my pillow, I prayed for God to come and save me, to let me die, or to kill the monster who continually hurt me. I screamed out to God as my mind drifted away.

I eventually turned my attention from God and found my relief, my sanctuary, in acid and pot. I found escape from my own personal hell by fleeing to the dark

TRUE VOL.2

44

streets where I would hang with kids like me: kids running from their own fears and their own doubts.

Not once did we see an angel come charging down the street, flaming sword raised above its head as it chopped down the demons of our home life. All we saw was the pusher as he passed a baggie to us. All we saw was that dark alley as we rolled a joint and passed it between us. All we saw were the dark hallucinations of our acid trips.

The words *I hate you* passed my lips every night as I tumbled into my bed, too drunk or stoned to move but alert enough to pray while I waited for my stepfather.

Then came the night when I finally felt God, finally caught a glimpse of an angel wing as he passed by.

As I stood there that night, listening to Dad rant and rave in his drunken rage, I knew God wasn't going to come save me. Dad was waving his hands in the air, a rifle clenched in his fist as he swore at me, "I'm going to ----ing kill you. I'm going to kill you and your mother."

My mother was safe in her new home, her new life. I was just an inconvenience sent off to live with my stepfather after I was arrested for holding. I hated her as much as I hated God. Unfortunately, hate was not saving me from the lunatic waving a loaded rifle at me.

My arms were already bruised where his hands had crushed them, and I could feel the tears running down my face. Dad dialed the phone and yelled into it, "If you pigs even think of coming up here, I'm going to kill my daughter."

I stood there, no longer afraid, waiting for his rage to end and for him to pass out, just like every other time. I flinched as I watched him walk toward me, his eyes lit up

with a gross light. He snarled at me and his spit sprayed my face. I felt like throwing up. He lifted up his large tanned hand with the back of it facing me and went to smack me but I jerked back, and his hand fell away. And then he turned toward the back door and walked out.

As my pulse started to come back, I heard a loud crack from the rifle. Dad walked into the house and picked up the phone he'd left on the countertop. "Did you hear that you [curse word, curse word]? The next one is for my daughter if you come here," he yelled.

I ran into my room. My terror finally took hold as I cried and prayed God would come and kill him. As the minutes turned into hours, as the noise turned to silence, I finally pulled myself up from the floor and walked out into the living room. Dad was passed out on the floor, rifle beside him and a loud snore erupting from his slack mouth. I could hear noise outside, and I looked between the blinds to see several cops talking. I watched as they piled back into their cruisers and pulled away. Obviously, the old drunk had quieted down enough for them to leave.

I stood there for a minute, watching my stepfather sleep. Hate filled me up; rage and terror drove me toward him and the rifle. I picked up that gun and looked at his face. I said a silent prayer to God, begging him to stop me. I pointed the barrel at my stepfather's chest, my finger resting on the trigger as I made sure the safety was off. I thought of all the pain and how it would end right there. Just as my finger was tightening around the trigger, I heard the word *don't* whispered softly in my ear. I suddenly felt as if something was tenderly holding me. This tenderness was so powerful it cut right through my rage and my determination to blow my stepdad off the face of the earth. I'd never experienced such powerful tenderness.

I slumped to my knees and started crying, the drunk beside me not even knowing I was there. I knew in the moment that no matter what, God loved me: I knew he was with me and didn't want me to become a murderer. I knew in that moment God's plan was for me to survive and succeed—and this wasn't the way to do it.

I moved away from my stepdad and flicked the safety on the rifle, setting it down away from him, and then I went to bed. For the first time I didn't say the words *I hate you*. For the first time I felt I was in the arms of love.

I finally fell asleep without fear.

My salvation didn't come for weeks after that, but I knew I had an angel by my side as I planned my escape.

I knew God was cheering me on and lending me his strength so I wouldn't fail.

I know although I've seen a glimpse of man's hell and the demons he has, God carried me and saved me. But I've fought hard to keep my faith in God. I've never told God I hate him again, but sometimes I've raged against him and demanded he explain why he let me be hurt—why he lets other children be hurt. Still, during those times I fall asleep dreaming of angels, and I hear the whispered words, "I have loved you always."

Sirena Van Schaik

HE IS A GOD OF DELIVERANCE

HE IS A GOD OF INFINITE SUPPORT.

"I will be your God throughout your lifetime—until your hair is white with age. I made you, and I will care for you. I will carry you along and save you."
—Isaiah 46:4, NLT

THE PLAIN FACT

"O Lord, you know all about this. Do not stay silent. Don't abandon me now, O Lord."

—Psalm 35:22, NLT

I sat on a soiled blue towel on the floor because the carpet was torn and the splintered wood beneath shone through. There were six or seven other people in the abandoned house my friend Matt lived in. The house, if it could even be called that, didn't have a bathroom or running water, and the kitchen floor had caved in. I was 21 years old, and I'd spent the last few nights sleeping on my dirty towel.

Our cocaine had run out several hours earlier, so we had switched to alcohol. I sat staring out the hole where a front door should've been. The sickly sound of gagging roused me from my daze, and I turned to see Matt lying face down in a puddle I quickly recognized as vomit. Before my mind had the chance to tell my body I was drunk and thus incapable of lifting a grown man, I grabbed Matt by the armpits and heaved him onto the stained mattress to my right. Once his vomiting had subsided, he touched my face sweetly and said, "Thanks, I think ya jus' saved my life." I think we had sex that night, but I don't remember for sure.

Six weeks earlier I'd been living in a spacious two-bedroom apartment on the north side of San Antonio, Texas. In the span of one week my boyfriend had died, causing me to lose my mind and as a result, my job. Soon I couldn't pay my bills, and I lost my apartment. Finally, I lost my faith.

"Friends" I'd known only a few months offered to let me stay with them, and that's when I agreed to do drugs for the first time in my life. Crank was the first drug to find its way up my nostril. I quickly took a liking to it and spent weeks at a time high. I didn't sleep. I didn't talk. I didn't go anywhere. All I did was write. I wrote in a journal. I wrote poems and songs. I wrote...and I cried.

I cried for the love I'd lost when my boyfriend was taken from me, but I also cried for myself. I was losing who I was, but I couldn't figure out how to change.

As the days passed, people came and went. I stayed. I barely heard the muffled sounds of laughter and conversation as I slipped deeper into myself. I stared at some electrical wires hanging out of the wall as the sounds around me grew louder and louder.

"JACKIE!" I turned at the sound of my name being yelled and my body being shaken.

"What?" I said barely above a whisper.

"I've been calling your name!" said a man whose name has escaped me. In fact, I'm not sure I ever knew his name.

"Sorry, what?" I answered, annoyed I had to talk.

"Did ya hear what we were talkin' 'bout? One of dem Jesus freaks came up to Rick at the liquor store and invited him to church. Can you imagine someone askin' this a--h-le to church lookin' the way he does? Amy here was telling us how you used to be, like, a good girl or something before you met us, and you even went to church and s--t. Do you buy into all that God stuff?"

"Yeah," I said without thinking.

"Awww, no s--t? Did we corrupt a sweet little church girl?" taunted Matt as his hand moved higher up my leg. I slapped his hand away. "Whatsa matter, baby? Don't you want some of this, or are ya too good for us all of a sudden?" He reached for me, but I stood before he could grab me.

"I'm going to take off. I could use some air," I said, moving toward the sheet we were using as a door.

"Come on, baby; don't go. We were jus' foolin' wit' ya. Don't take everythang so personal all da time."

"I'm just going to take a walk." I darted outside, walked a few feet, and ran smack into my car. I think I'd forgotten I even had a car. I found the key in my pocket, and I got in my car and drove. That day I moved back in with my mom.

I'd moved all my things into her place when I lost my apartment, so I used my key and went into my old room and slept for 20 hours. I woke up feeling sober for the first time in months. I paced my room. I stopped to gaze at the pictures framed on my dresser. I picked up each picture—my family, my childhood friends, my dog—each one made me smile with happy memories. But as I moved down the row of pictures to the ones from youth group, my smile faded. I looked at my smiling face surrounded by my church friends laughing and hugging me. One picture was from the day I became a Christian at a state youth conference; another was of us at the beach.

53

There we were at the bowling alley, at a car wash, at a barbecue.

With one pass I knocked the pictures off my dresser, and they landed with a crash on the floor. I screamed out to God, "All those years of church and Sunday school and youth group and choir. What was all that for? Where are you now?" I dropped to my knees and violently sobbed into my hands. I cried myself back to sleep.

When I woke, nothing had miraculously changed. My life was still the same, but I felt calmer somehow, so I picked the pictures up off the floor and placed them back on the dresser. None had broken. But what God did for me that day was even more surprising, and it changed my life. He helped me get up, get dressed, eat breakfast, call an old friend, and read a book. The next day God got me out of bed and dressed once again—and then the day after that.

I'd like to say I never slipped again, but that's simply not true. There were days when I still felt gripped with despair and even days when I found comfort in a white, powdery substance. That day wasn't the first I fell to my knees sobbing.

But slowly, I felt drawn to the Bible for comfort. I started praying again and reading the books I loved. I started talking to people. I got a job. I starting painting again and writing for fun. I laughed easily and smiled often. I looked forward to the future.

I fell to my knees again, but not in contempt or despair this time. I felt gratitude and thanksgiving. I'm thankful every day that my Father welcomed me back into his arms without question or judgment and that I can let go of that chapter in my life without shame.

I finally came to terms with the plain fact that God hadn't abandoned me. I'd abandoned him.

Jackie Abruzzini

THE NEW GIRL

—Matthew 10:32, LB

Mom brought our rusty Chevy to a stop in front of the looming blue sign with gold lettering: "Welcome to Linden High School—you're in Lion Country!" The snarling lions on the sign didn't look very welcoming. Neither did the kids milling around in the parking lot. They gawked at our old clunker as if it were a time machine that had landed in the middle of their upscale neighborhood. I wished it were—then at least we could travel back to when Mom had a job, I had a father, and we had a home.

Somewhere a bell rang, so I took a deep breath and got out of the car.

Mom said, "Don't worry; you'll do fine. I'll call you later, okay?"

I nodded. I wouldn't see her for a week. I moved in with my grandparents when Dad left, and we lost our house. Mom spent her days searching for a job and her

evenings house-sitting for a friend out of town. We saw each other only on weekends.

The worst part for me was switching to a new school, but like everything else in my life then, I had no choice in the matter. I forced a smile and waved as Mom drove away, the Chevy's tailpipe belching black smoke.

As I made my way through the crowd of designer jeans and handbags, I was keenly aware of my thrift-store clothes and shabby backpack. Stares pierced me like needles when I entered my homeroom. To my horror the first thing the teacher did was call me to the front of the class.

I felt as if I were the sideshow attraction and Mr. Roose was the carnival barker. *"Step right up, folks, and see The New Girl! That's right, a creature so hideous even her own father ran away! Notice the faded sweater unraveling at the sleeve! Observe the jeans so worn in the knees they could tear at any moment! See the hair badly in need of a trim! No, folks, your noses don't deceive you—that's cheap drugstore perfume she's wearing! Come one, come all..."*

What he actually said was, "Everyone, this is Tiffany. She transferred from Fremont High in Stockton. Glad to have you, Tiffany."

Twenty-nine bored faces looked at me. One girl rolled her eyes. As I walked back to my seat, she whispered in another girl's ear, and then they both burst into giggles. My face was on fire. I willed myself not to blink, to keep the tears brimming in my eyes from spilling. *Oh, God, please just let me survive today.*

I uttered that plea in desperation to a vague Jesus I barely knew. I had no idea how real he would become to me.

My life at Linden High was a nightmare. It didn't take long to learn the only thing worse than being the new girl in school is being the poor new girl in a rich school. Things weren't much better outside of class: My grandmother made a point of letting me know I was a burden. One night I started reading a children's Bible I had—a gift from a Sunday school teacher when I was in third grade. I came across a passage where Jesus is describing the power of prayer. I was amazed. *Could I really move mountains if I believed?* I decided to give prayer a serious try.

I felt like I'd found a magic lamp! As God granted one request after another, my faith grew, and my relationship with him became stronger. Then I got a call from Mom. I could hear the excitement in her voice, and I knew my most fervent prayer had been answered. "I got a job! It's just minimum wage, but I think we can afford a small apartment. You can go back to Fremont."

Mom gave me the only bedroom in our new place, and she slept on the sofa. I made friends and actually enjoyed going to school. Even my grades improved—straight A's in every subject. It became clear God let me go through some rough times so I could meet him and better appreciate the blessings he had in store for me.

There was just one problem. My experience as the Linden High School leper had given me a deep insecurity. I didn't want to be an outcast again, and I feared being labeled as a "holy roller," a "Jesus freak." I convinced myself God understood. So what if I didn't go around wearing "I Love Jesus" T-shirts? He knew what was in my heart, and that's all that mattered. I was right about one thing—God did know my heart, and he knew I valued others' acceptance more than I valued his acceptance.

I still prayed, squeezing in time for God whenever I could—changing for gym, walking between classes, waiting in the snack bar line.

One day before an English quiz I made sure no one was looking, and then I bowed my head, closed my eyes, and prayed for help with the test. When I opened my eyes and looked up, my heart froze.

Looking right at me was Nathan Banks—the cutest guy I'd ever seen in real life. Let me put it this way: When I wasn't praying and thinking about God, I was usually thinking about Nathan.

The first time Nathan had glanced my way, and he'd busted me praying!

"Did you just say a prayer?"

The classroom was quiet. He might as well have shouted through a bullhorn.

My lips felt glued together. I thought, *Open your mouth, stupid! Say something witty! Deny it!*

Out loud I said, "Huh?" Brilliant.

Everyone was paying attention now. Nathan said, "I saw you close your eyes and mouth something about Jesus. You were praying."

My heart was thumping so loudly I was sure people could hear it. While I tried to find my voice, Nathan said, "Hey, it's cool. There's nothing wrong with that."

I still wanted to deny it and save my image. Then I pictured Jesus sitting there, waiting to see if I would deny him after all he'd done for me.

"Yeah. Yeah, I guess I was praying. I'm a Christian."

Nathan smiled. "So that's how you get those good grades. Would you say a prayer for me? I didn't read the book!"

Everyone laughed, but they weren't laughing at me. I was worried for nothing.

Christ never promised his followers popularity—quite the opposite. But what he did promise is if we acknowledge him before others, he'll acknowledge us before his Father in heaven.

How cool will that be?

Tiffany O'Neill

THANK YOU, FOZZIE

—Ezekiel 34:26

She was a horrible waitress—never got anybody's order right, always screwed up something on the customers' bills so they had to complain to the manager. She had stains all over her gaudy pink uniform and runs in her stockings, and her bright-red wiry hair and pickle nose planted right in the middle of her oval face made her look just like that lovable Muppet Fozzie Bear. Only this Fozzie wasn't quite so lovable. Or so I thought...

It was Thanksgiving night, and no one else wanted to work, so it was just Fozzie and me slinging molded turkey shavings and ice cream scoops of mashed potatoes to the clusters of senior citizens who stumbled in out of the brisk November cold.

We'd never talked much, and tonight was no exception. The diner had already started with the Christmas carols, and Fozzie sang right along all night. I tried to share her enthusiasm, but I had troubles of my own. My father's business was in disarray, and he was considering bankruptcy. After my parents' divorce my mother had

moved to an oceanfront condominium way beyond her means. It'd been for sale for a year, and no one had even attempted a bite at her ludicrous asking price. My life felt out of control, and I had no one to turn to. With so many troubles of their own, how could I politely remind my parents they'd always offered to help pay for my college tuition?

I'd been slaving away at the diner for nearly a year now, trying to save up enough for my first semester at the local state university. I was almost there. And then one morning my car didn't start. I soon learned the entire electrical system was faulty. It would cost over $900 to fix.

"Nine hundred dollars?" I heard someone reply. I blinked my eyes and stared into Fozzie's solemn face. "And just when you were so close to starting college, too. Not a very happy Thanksgiving, is it?"

Had I really said all of my troubles out loud? And had Fozzie actually...listened? But there we were, chatting quietly over two cups of mudlike diner coffee as the last few customers of the evening wandered out into the miserable cold.

"Thank you," I said humbly, feeling a lump in my throat at having judged Fozzie so badly. "Thank you for listening. I didn't mean to go on like that."

"Well, now," she sighed, "it doesn't sound like there's much listening going on in your house these days. Everybody's rushing around with their own problems. Sometimes a friendly ear can change the way you think about things."

She was right. Pouring out my troubles, things I hadn't even told my best friends for fear of embarrassment, had left me feeling as if I'd just had a restful night's sleep.

"Listen," she said as we finished our side work and clocked out. "I've been trying to sell my old car for weeks. It's in good shape. Now it's not exactly a babe magnet, but...I'm only asking $500 for it. That's less than it would take to fix your car. Maybe the money you save would round out what you need for tuition."

"And then some," I gasped, leaping at the offer like a little kid.

We sat quietly on the way to her apartment, the only two on the bus. Everyone else was busy celebrating the holiday with family and friends. I thought of my mom at her annual gala Thanksgiving dinner party at the country club, despite the fact she'd had to borrow money from my grandmother to pay for the ticket. And my dad working double time at his company to try and make things right. Neither of them had even bothered to ask me what I'd be doing for the holiday.

Fozzie's car was an 11-year-old Honda with just a little rust and nearly new tires. Its paint job was faded, and the interior was worn, but it turned over in an instant and purred like a kitten. There were over 100,000 miles on the car, but it was in better shape than the one I was planning on having fixed. I couldn't believe my good luck.

"The paperwork's upstairs," said Fozzie. "You wait here and I'll go get it. I'm sure you have big plans for tonight. I wouldn't want to keep you."

I watched sadly as Fozzie slowly walked away from me. She favored one leg, and the soles of her dollar-store shoes looked old and worn. The halls of her building were dark and quiet, and I'd picked up enough clues so far

HE IS A GOD OF INFINITE SUPPORT

to determine Fozzie wasn't exactly walking into a festive apartment tonight, either.

It didn't take long to catch up to her. Her smile filled the corridor as we opened her door, and she fumbled through a cheap desk for the car's paperwork. I sat on a threadbare couch and looked around her one-bedroom apartment while she searched. The room was clean and cozy. The table was set with a paper tablecloth bearing turkeys and pilgrims. Turkey candles and pilgrim saltshakers rounded out her festive holiday decorations.

"Oh, I'm sorry," I said, seeing the table set for two and getting up. "I didn't realize you were expecting company."

Fozzie smiled sadly, looking at her wishful attempts to bring the holidays into her home. "Oh no," she sighed. "That's just habit. Ever since my husband died six years ago, I can't stand to see a table set for one. I just leave two plates out so people don't go feeling sorry for me. I don't even know why I bothered this year," she added, handing me the car's title as I wrote her a check for $500. "You don't need to set a table for take-out Chinese food."

I looked around the room at the shabby furniture and homemade curtains. Scattered about were photographs of several young men and women in various celebratory poses: graduations, promotions, and birthdays. Younger versions of Fozzie were standing nearby, smiling proudly. Where were her children this holiday night? Just then my stomach rumbled. I'd been too upset all night even to think about food. Now I was suddenly starving.

"Listen," I said, pulling out the wad of ones and fives from my shift at the diner. "I had a pretty good night. Why don't I order us some take-out so your nice table here doesn't go to waste? My treat. It's the least I can do to thank you for bailing me out like this."

Fozzie couldn't find the phone fast enough.

Later, as Fozzie showed off the interior of the car and its impressive features, most of which no longer worked, I noticed the stains on her uniform and felt an aching in my heart. Her kind and generous gesture had afforded me the opportunity to finally start college on time. Classes would start soon; I'd move away from home and once settled, find a cushy job on campus and start the process of financial aid and student loans. My long, hard nights of dishing up buttered carrots and creamed spinach were nearly at an end. I wondered how many long, hard *years* Fozzie would have to work before she could finally retire. I pondered how Fozzie had come to my rescue, but I thought maybe, just maybe, she wasn't alone.

I'd heard God works in mysterious ways. So many of my family members, so-called friends, and relatives had turned deaf ears to my troubles. But here was Fozzie—a stranger really, with less than two cents to rub together, a run-down apartment on the wrong side of town, and a family who didn't really care about her either—answering my prayers. Who knew the worst waitress in the world would turn out to be the very best angel?

Driving away in my "new" used car toward a bright future, thanks to the kind acts of a Muppet angel, I ran over a bump, and the faulty glove box door swung open. Inside was a thin envelope. I opened it at a stoplight and then pulled over until my tears dried up and I could see the road again.

"Thank you for the first Thanksgiving I've celebrated in six years," said a quickly scrawled note on cheap stationery. "This isn't much, but it's all the tips I made tonight. Maybe you can buy one of your textbooks on me. Thanks again, Mavis."

"Mavis," I thought, finally pulling back onto the road. All those nights together, and it was sitting right there on her nametag the whole time: "Mavis."

I counted the money in the envelope. There was enough there for two textbooks.

There was also just enough for a brand-new uniform for Mavis.

Rusty Fischer

STRANDED

> *"The Lord will command his angels to take good care of you."*
>
> —Psalm 91:11, NIrV

Pow! Screech! I struggled to maintain control of my car. The steering wheel violently shook in my hands. I'd only been driving a year, but I knew that sound wasn't good. It felt like a tire blew. I turned the wheel with every muscle in my upper body to direct the car toward the side of the road.

Mom had warned me not to drive back to college so late. I jumped out of the car and checked the tires. The back driver's-side tire was shredded. I wondered what could have done that.

There I sat, stranded on a pitch-black freeway. Mom's words about waiting until morning to drive back echoed in my head. Every 10 minutes or so a car zoomed by and rocked my tilted car.

Pulling together my courage, I hopped out, telling myself I could change the tire. My stepdad had taught me how to do it. He wanted to make sure I could take care of

myself. I popped the trunk and grabbed the crowbar and spare tire. No problem.

I placed the crowbar over the lug nuts on the wheel rim and pulled, then pushed. They didn't budge. I even frantically jumped up and down on the crowbar. Nothing. I remembered when the mechanic put new tires on the week before, he'd used an electric machine to tighten the lug nuts. "They're too *tight*," I said through clenched teeth as I gave it one last push. "Now what?" I mumbled.

"God," I prayed, "I know I've been busy lately and have slacked on my prayers, but this is getting a little scary. I don't have a way to contact anyone, I can't get the tire changed, and I'm alone on a dark freeway. Please help me."

I glanced across the four lanes and spotted a few homes in the distance. Clouds began to cover the moon, which made it harder to see anything. The streetlight I'd stopped under was burned out.

"Just my luck," I muttered. I scrambled toward the homes and stumbled into a ditch of stinky sewage water. Muddy water squished into my shoes and soaked my socks. I waved my hand over my face. The smell was awful. I trudged out of the mess and straight into a fence at least 12 feet high. Barbed wire circled the top of it. There was no way I could scale the fence. If I did make it, the barbed wire would slice me to pieces.

What is this place, a prison? I wondered, peering at the grounds. But it appeared to be a country club or private development.

The other side of the freeway had massive cornfields that stretched for miles. So it wasn't likely I'd find help there.

Breathe, Jenn, breathe, I told myself as panic set in.

Back at the car I tried to loosen the lug nuts one more time. They still didn't move. Tears flooded my eyes, blurring my vision.

"God, make it move! Please help me!" I shouted.

When I realized I was totally out of luck, I jumped back in the car and just lost control. I sat there and sobbed for at least a half hour. A few cars whizzed by every so often, and I was tempted to try and flag one down but came to the same conclusion I had when I'd first discovered the tire was flat: It just wasn't safe. The past week there was a story in the local paper about a huge rock that had broken a girl's car windshield. The two men who stopped to "help" raped and killed her. Frantic thoughts raced in my mind. I huddled in the front seat praying and crying.

Then it started to rain...hard.

"Just wonderful," I smirked. "A rainstorm. How about a little thunder and lightning, too, since I'm afraid of thunderstorms?" Lightning streaked in the distance and thunder cracked. I jumped in my seat. The one thing I don't like about spring—storms.

Suddenly, two lights reflected in my rearview mirror. My heart began pounding so loud my ears rang. I scrunched down in the seat, praying that God had sent me a cop. No luck. A burly man stepped out of his car and headed toward me, pausing briefly to look at the flat tire. He cupped his hands over his face and peered into the window.

"Do you need some help?" he yelled.

I didn't answer or move. I didn't even breathe. *This is it. I'm dead,* I thought.

"I see you tried changing your tire. You're smart for staying in the car and keeping the doors locked and windows up," he shouted above the thunder and rain.

Still not sure if I should trust him, I peeked at him. His big, brown eyes looked gentle as a puppy's. They gave off a feeling of warmth. He even had a glow around him like an angel. Rubbing my eyes, I convinced myself it was just the moon slipping out from behind the clouds. Yet it was still storming.

"Listen, I'm going to go ahead and change the tire. Stay put," he said.

"Where would I go?" I muttered, my stomach queasy from the night's events.

The car jiggled as he struggled with the lug nuts like I had. In my side mirror I could see he was getting soaked. His wet hair was plastered on his head. His raincoat hood drooped, full of water, and emptied down his back. *Poor man,* I thought. But I was not about to get out of the car and offer him a towel even though I had one in the back seat.

A bit later he tapped on the window. "All done. You're safe now," he beamed. "Now go straight to your dorm and be careful."

I mouthed "thank you" and noticed I was still shaking when I started the engine. How did he know I was on my way to college? My laundry baskets and food bags in the back seat were dead giveaways, along with the college mascot sticker plastered in my back window. But there was something about the way he said it. His tone was very loving and caring. I wished I could jump out and give him a hug.

"Get going," he urged. "I'm going to follow you to the university exit; you'll be fine from there. Go slow on that spare tire and get it changed tomorrow, first thing."

Driving the rest of the way to school, a peace settled over me. God had answered my prayers and sent someone to take care of me. I prayed and thanked God for sending me a guardian angel in the form of a man.

Glancing in the rearview mirror to give him a quick wave as I exited the freeway, I froze. No car was behind me. In fact, no other car was on the road. I looked over my shoulder. My car was the only one in sight. Instantly, my hair stood up on my arms and my neck.

"No way," I whispered.

Jenna King

CARRIED BY THE GOOD SHEPHERD

—Psalm 121:7

I heard if a lamb tends to stray, a shepherd might break its leg and hold it close until the leg heals. By then the lamb knows how much the shepherd cares and never wants to leave him.

I was born with several hemangiomas—tumors consisting of blood vessels. The largest one was on my left arm from wrist to elbow. Hemangiomas start as red marks. They swell bigger for the first few months and then start receding.

Shortly before I was born, my parents moved across the country to stay temporarily with my mom's parents, "Omommy" and "Pempa." We're all sure God put my parents there at that time because Omommy was a registered nurse. Omommy helped my mom change my dressings each day. She knew just what to do and could handle it when blood sometimes shot from a tumor when the bandages were removed.

On top of this I had colic. So Mom, Dad, and Omommy took turns rocking me and walking the floor with me. Omommy sometimes sang or recited the 23rd Psalm to me. She continued to do this throughout her life.

I was also born with a kidney valve that didn't close properly, causing recurring infections. To battle this problem I was on antibiotics for five years, and one of the common side effects is epilepsy.

So when I was five, I started having 20 to 25 seizures a day. At that point the doctors said I'd probably outgrow it. We experimented with many medications (one left me color-blind), but none completely controlled my seizures. Through every test my parents were with me while others prayed for me. I have to say as tough as it was, at least I never felt alone.

When I turned 18, I stopped seeing my pediatrician and begin going to an adult neurologist. For years my pediatrician had told me I was not qualified for corrective brain surgery. However, my new doctor thought I was a wonderful candidate for the operation. Although I was excited to learn there was hope for my condition, I also became really nervous after watching a film about the brain surgery I'd undergo. I found out the patient remains awake through the entire process.

But I became less nervous and more excited with every visit to the surgeon. The thought of never having another seizure, or even having a decreased number, was so awesome. So I continued through the process and went through the many tests I had to take before I could proceed to the operating room. As the day of surgery came nearer, I felt more afraid, but I knew I had prayer support, and I was in my shepherd's [God's] hands. God had supported me by giving me great parents and many caring people throughout my life to pray for me. I knew

if I placed myself in his hands, everything would turn out well whether the surgery worked or not, even if I ended up with nerve damage.

The stretcher rolled into the prep room on the morning of my first surgery, and my nerves quivered. I had to have two different operations: The first one was to insert a device to monitor the electrical activity in my brain for a few weeks so they'd know exactly where to operate. I lay there staring at the flickering fluorescent lights and listened to my doctors and nurses tell me about the surgery. A sharp pain shot up my arm as they injected the anesthetic and rolled me into the O.R.

I lay on the operating table, shivering as a constant cool breeze blew on my face. Holding the hand of my speech pathologist, I prayed God would give me peace through the next few hours. I felt no pain through the surgery, just the irritating slurping of the suction above my right ear. "Fifteen more minutes," the surgeon said to the anesthesiologist. I floated in and out of consciousness.

After surgery I was violently ill from the anesthesia, and I struggled to sleep. My boyfriend Maverick brushed my hand with a gentle kiss. I felt tickles on my fingertips as Dad helped me relax.

Sunlight peeked through my window when I awoke the next morning. I knew there'd be some swelling, but when I looked in the mirror, I thought, *Oh no, Maverick is coming, and my face looks like a pillow! Oh well, there's nothing I can do about it.*

For 12 days I lay in bed with wires hooked directly to my brain. Many times over I thought, *I hope this is worth it!*

Then it was time for the final operation. Excitement rushed through me this time, and I wasn't as nervous as

I was before the first operation. I felt as though God had held my hand through the first one, and I trusted he'd do it again.

Before the surgery the doctors said I'd remember nothing. Yet vivid memories still play through my mind. A strange tickling sensation moved in my head, and the urge to squirm was so great I could hardly contain myself. I wanted to get up and run away. But I prayed through it, and although the six-hour surgery was terrible, I felt the strange peace I'd prayed for.

The next day I experienced several seizures. One was so severe my vital signs stopped for a few seconds. Doctors and nurses ran to revive me. The specialists informed my parents seizures were a natural reaction to brain surgery, and it didn't mean the operation wasn't successful.

My mom stayed with me in the hospital day and night for 24 days. My dad, sister, and other family and friends came when possible. My room filled with cards, balloons, and gifts. One nurse proclaimed, "Are you a celebrity?" My aunt and uncle sent me a stuffed lamb. When I opened the package, it reminded me once again, "The Lord is my shepherd."

A few days later the doctors and surgeons sat at the foot of my bed. "The brain matter was affected in two areas," they informed us. "We removed the one that was the main trigger of the seizures. Probably the other spot will remain quiet."

Through the next 10 days I was seizure-free, so they removed the head wrap and sent me home.

Now, six months later, I haven't had one seizure. The doctors wanted to keep me on full doses of my medications for an entire year, but I struggled with severe dizzy spells and feeling as if I lived in pea soup—foggy and in

slow motion. So my doctors decreased the doses, and I'm still seizure-free.

Part of my brain is missing, but nobody has noticed any difference. (I'm not sure if that's a compliment or an insult.)

I praise God for everything he's brought me through. He held me close and never let me out of his sight. I could feel God even through the worst moments of my hardest trials. I can't imagine what it would've been like to go through all of this without knowing without a doubt God cares for me and will never leave me.

Now I'm looking forward to driving, attending college, and getting a job. All those things will take some major adjustments and effort, but I figure if God could successfully get me through major brain surgery, he can get me through anything.

Katherine Knickerbocker

A FLICKER OF HOPE

> *"And hope does not disappoint us, because God has poured out his love into our hearts by the Holy Spirit, whom he has given us."*

—Romans 5:5

I watched her as she looked at me, and our eyes met again. She looked sad and I couldn't blame her. *You really are a nobody,* I thought as I stared at her. *No one really wants to be your friend, and, after all, why should they? You aren't really worth knowing in the first place.*

Tears welled up in my eyes as I glanced away from the mirror. I placed my hands over my ears to try to shut out the negative thoughts. Shaking my head, I tried to dismiss the condescending voice. I was discouraged by the girl reflected in the glass, the image that echoed hopelessness and low self-esteem. Before I could catch another glimpse of myself, I flipped off the light and left the room, hoping my thoughts would leave as well. But I knew they'd never go away. I knew I'd never have any peace of mind. These thoughts were my constant companions, lurking in the shadows of my mind, waiting to attack me in my weakest moments. It was a battle I was never going to win, a battle against clinical depression.

I shuffled across the old worn carpet of my college dorm room floor, faded by the pacing feet of many anxious students before my time. Wandering to the single small window, I rested my head against the rusty paneling and peered outside. The sky was beginning to darken—a sure sign of coming rain. A cloudy day. Go figure. A dark and dreary day to match my dark and dreary thoughts. My eyes shifted to a group of college students making their way across the green lawn. Suddenly, the heavens opened wide, and a shower of sweet-smelling rain poured down. Squealing with excitement, the students began chasing each other around in the rain, delighted by the surprise.

Sighing, I desperately wished for what they could so easily experience with the coming rain—joy. Laughter. A happiness in feeling fully alive. Tears began to pour like the rain, streaming down my face as the desire of my heart surged within me. *Didn't they know there were people like me who couldn't enjoy what was meant to be enjoyed? Didn't they know pessimism plagued me like a disease?* Oh, how I wanted to be like them. But I felt as though I was alone. No one seemed to want to hear about what was going on inside me.

My eyes fell on a picture of a group of smiling girls, arms wrapped around each others' shoulders. The picture was black and white, its frame at home on the rusty windowsill. Feelings of loneliness rose within me. I'd confided in them, and they'd responded with blank stares. I'd revealed my struggle with depression, and instead of being helpful, they became uncomfortable and left me with the statement: "It'll be okay."

But it wasn't okay.

"Where are you, God?" I barely whispered, gazing up at the gloomy sky. My question was answered with a thunderous reply. Eyes downcast, I sank to the floor.

Where was God in all of this? I felt as though he'd abandoned me, too. Was I being punished for something I'd done? I shook my head as if to answer my own question. It wasn't in God's character to punish me like this for my sins. God is full of love and compassion, always quick to forgive, and slow to get angry. Yet the two-year battle was wearing thin on my soul.

"Please, God," I begged softly, "heal me from this depression. I don't know what else to do, and I can't bear it any longer. Only you can help me—no one else will." Desperate for relief, I held my head in my hands, resting against the cold and calloused wall.

I sat there for what seemed like hours, silently praying God would come to my rescue. A loud ringing interrupted my thoughts. After a few seconds I recognized the noise as the phone and quickly rose to answer it. Pulling the black cordless from its cradle, I placed the receiver to my ear.

"Hello?" I struggled to answer.

"Hey," came a comforting voice on the other end. I recognized it as a friend from school I hadn't seen or heard from in a while. For some reason I'd felt comfortable enough with him to share my struggle over an e-mail.

"I was wondering," he continued, "if you'd like to get together tonight and talk about some of the things you've been dealing with."

"I'd love to," I eagerly responded, promising to meet him later for a bonfire and conversation.

That night we met behind the old student center, firewood in hand. The rain had long since gone, and the firewood was dry and perfect for burning. We struck matches, and the fire grew, blazing brightly. The two of

us sat on two logs. And our thoughts gently formed into words as we shared one heart. The light from the fire cast a soft glow on his face, revealing the deep concern he had for me. He listened intently as I poured from my heart all the frustration and heartache I'd been silently dealing with over the years. The more I spoke, the more gentle his demeanor became. He didn't seem uncomfortable at all. That night he spoke words of encouragement, of hope, of strength, and of love: God's love. From one soul to another the power of God moved as the fire dwindled to glowing embers and finally gray ash. We stayed until the first morning light appeared over the horizon and dawn began to approach. Parting company, he left with the promise to pray and stand by me through the good times and bad—a promise he never forgot. And I left with warmth in my heart.

As I walked back to my dorm, the sun's first rays smiled on me. A peace came upon my heart and mind. God hadn't abandoned me. In fact, he'd always been taking care of me and only asked for my faith in return. Though I knew a slow process of healing awaited me, I no longer had to fear. I'd been given hope. I'd been rescued. God had given me the support I needed at the time I needed it most.

He'd sent me a friend.

Rachel Giffin

TIME AND AGAIN

It was already dark outside since it was 5:45 on a winter's evening. I needed to make a deposit at my bank and I knew that I wouldn't have time the following day when the bank opened. I pulled into the lot and parked near the ATM machine. I was already late for a meeting and as I went to grab a pen to fill out the deposit slip, I couldn't find one. That was not only frustrating but really weird because I always have several pens in my car and in my purse. I guess I just have this thing about having a pen around at all times. So, I scrambled around the car praying, "Lord, help me find a pen. Help me find a pen!" As I was feeling around between the seats, I noticed this light shining into the car at me through the passenger window.

Now my bank is located in a business area, so on a Sunday, the place is usually pretty deserted. This kind of concerned me as I drove in—I was alone and didn't have my cell phone with me. As I squinted, trying to see through the light that was pointed at my head, I made out the image of a man dressed in dark clothes. I cracked my window just slightly so that in case it was a security guard or someone in need of help, I could hear.

What I heard wasn't at all what I was expecting. Out of this man's mouth came a repetitive demand for me to get out of my car because, according to him, he needed a woman right there and then. He both propositioned me and threatened me as he very specifically told me the plans he had for me and all about what he was going to do to me.

I couldn't see if he had a weapon, but I wasn't about to find out. I turned the engine of the car over and put the transmission in reverse. As I backed out of the spot, he started chasing me. I pushed down on the accelerator and got out of there as fast as I could. I shook from the shock and terror of it all the way to my meeting.

The next morning I got into my car to report to jury duty when I looked over and couldn't miss the sight of three pens right there on the passenger seat, lined up in a perfect row. I thought, *No way!* Immediately God spoke to my spirit and said, "I hid them from you! I knew if you found a pen then you would have filled out the deposit slip and left the car! And that man would have hurt you. It was my protection on you."

During lunch break for jury duty, I decided to take a walk in the neighborhood adjacent to the courthouse. I had walked a few blocks when I got this creepy feeling that someone was following me. I turned around and there was a man in a truck that had slowed down as he approached me. *What?* I thought to myself. *Am I a weirdo magnet or something? What's going on?*

I picked up my pace as I looked around for a house with a car in the driveway or some sign of life around me. I began walking faster and noticed that there was a small shopping center a short way up the block. I nearly made it to the entrance of the center, but the man in the truck turned right in front of me and cut me off, half an inch from hitting me! He sat in his truck staring at me with this smirk on his face.

Looking around in a panic, I noticed a man standing on the corner. I could tell that he had noticed what was going on and looked concerned. He shot the guy in the truck a dirty look and came up to me, asking if he could help me get to where I was going. I hesitantly walked in his direction, and he walked a bit ahead of me, it seemed so that I would feel safer. I bent down to tie my shoe, and he stopped ahead of me on the sidewalk as he patiently waited for me to begin walking again. Eventually I decided that it would be all right to catch up with him.

When I did, he asked if I was heading anywhere in particular. I said that I had just been looking for a place to get a bite to eat. He motioned me to follow him and then led me to a small restaurant where I ordered something to eat. The man ordered and sat at a table next to me. He waited patiently as I ate and seemed to be watching out for me. When I was finished, he said that he would walk me back. I quickly responded, "I'll be okay," but I immediately heard God say, "I want you to know that my protection is on you. If it means hiding pens or sending someone to protect you, I am with you."

I was totally overwhelmed with God's hand in these situations. But these were not the only times that he had done something like that for me.

Once in South Africa, God miraculously kept a band of men who had broken into the children's home where I was serving from entering again. The week prior, the home had been broken into three times. This time, they had come back with guns, and as they attempted to break a lock to get inside, they for some weird reason couldn't. It was in a gated community on a gated property and the door to the house had an additional gate in front of it. They had gotten through all the security gates and were trying to break the lock of the wooden door—the only thing separating me and the three burglars! I was paralyzed in fear. I couldn't run even if I tried, so I sat up in bed and began praying. I could hear them getting frustrated as they struggled with the lock. After a while, I heard them give up and walk away.

The following morning after a basically sleepless night, I was about to e-mail my support group back home and ask them to please kick up the prayers for our protection. Instead I opened an e-mail that had come in the night. It was from a friend who said that she had been going about her day in California when she suddenly felt led to pray for me. She said she finally felt released from needing to pray because she got a sense that "nothing could get through."

"Do you have any idea what that would mean?" she wondered. I e-mailed her back to let her know just how powerful her prayers of intervention had been.

Another time, I was in Mozambique serving with a team of volunteers in a remote area that served as a dump. We had been offering medical attention to the local people when these guys kept harassing me. Finally I walked out of the area, trying to get away from them. Unfortunately, they found me. Three of the guys approached me and very quickly grabbed my arms and began dragging me away.

I began screaming and calling out to one of the guys in our group. He obviously didn't hear me, and by this point they had dragged me a bit far. Suddenly, this tall man came out of nowhere and managed to get them off me. There were three of them and only one of him, but he grabbed me away from them and quickly led me to a car that was waiting with some of the people from my group. I fell into the back seat and pushed myself upright to turn and thank him, but he was nowhere to be seen. That tall man, with virtually nowhere to hide, was gone from sight.

God came through for me those times in Africa; he did it again at the ATM, and then, the very next day on break for jury duty, he again ensured me that he was looking out for me.

I have recently committed to opening an orphanage in Tanzania. I'm just barely out of college, and the adventures and trials that lie ahead are yet to be seen. But I will go into that calling with complete confidence, knowing that time and again, God has demonstrated his unwavering protection and support in my life.

God's definitely got my back.

Anonymous

HE IS A GOD OF TRANSFORMATION.

"Don't copy the behavior and customs of this world, but let God transform you into a new person by changing the way you think. Then you will know what God wants you to do, and you will know how good and pleasing and perfect his will really is."
—Romans 12:2, NLT

DIFFERENT

> *"However, I consider my life worth nothing to me, if only I may finish the race and complete the task the Lord Jesus has given me—the task of testifying to the gospel of God's grace."*

—Acts 20:24

God: The concept that God exists or what he might be like if he did exist never made its way into my thoughts while I was growing up. I never attended any church when I was a kid, except on special occasions when my mom, who grew up Catholic, would make me go. It all seemed very ceremonial more than anything, and I didn't really get it. I never understood the concept of Easter or anything much—except Jesus was born on December 25 and you got presents on Christmas. Cool.

My mom raised me, and my dad was never in the picture. So I was very much influenced by her and the way she went about life, which was basically going to work and coming home. She was not what you'd call really social. That's how I assumed all people lived and didn't think twice about living the same way. I went to school and went home right after. Although I thought it was normal, it meant I never made many friends.

Living like this, which seemed pointless and boring, often made me wonder why people chose to live when they weren't particularly happy. I wondered why we all bothered when there wasn't much joy. It seemed like a lot of work for no good reason.

Then I'd see people trying to numb the pain of life by doing drugs and alcohol, and I really wondered about the point of living if so many people were so miserable they tried to numb life. Living just didn't seem to make sense.

So when I was a freshman in high school, I decided to kill myself.

All I could think about was being done with this life since it just didn't seem worthwhile. I devised a plan to take some pills and check out once and for all. The only problem was I woke up the next morning. I was still here. That was a major disappointment. Plus I experienced terrible physical pain as a result.

As I progressed through high school, I tried to kill myself in a number of different ways, obviously without success.

By my senior year I'd finally made some friends. The thought of killing myself then made me feel kind of bad. I thought if my friends really cared, which they seemed to, it'd be awful for them if I did something like that. But I just couldn't buy into believing I had any real future or purpose.

Toward the end of my senior year I decided I'd just end it all after graduation. As that time approached and I thought about how my friends were going to feel, I decided to write notes to some of them. I wanted them to know how much they'd meant to me.

Well, I guess the way I worded things made them suspect I might be planning suicide. So to try to get someone to help me or at least keep me from hurting myself, they told my counselor, who notified the police. The police showed up at my school and detained me until they figured out where to send me for further help.

I ended up being taken to a mental hospital where I was given a psychiatric evaluation. Certain I didn't want to end up staying there, I pretty much told them what they wanted to hear. I convinced them I'd just wanted some attention. So they released me but put me under house arrest for a few months, which meant I wasn't allowed to go anywhere the summer after I graduated.

One day I was lying in bed, thinking back on my life, and I wondered why it wasn't easier just to end it all. *Why do I have to go through so much trouble just to die? Why am I still here?*

That same night I had a strange but very profound sense there actually was a purpose for my being. I had a feeling something was trying to keep me alive. These thoughts made me want to pursue things that might help explain why life might be worthwhile.

For the first time I considered the possibility of a God who created everything for some purpose. I took the only course of action I knew to explore this concept and started going to the church I'd occasionally attended while growing up. I soon discovered I couldn't relate to what they did there, so I made a decision to seek out others to help me find some answers.

A friend of mine named Seth had been going to meetings at this guy's house where they got together to "worship" God. My mom brought me up thinking people like that were kind of weird, so even though Seth invited me many times to go with him, I turned him down time

and again. It just sounded like a cult thing to me, once I heard they met in a house and not in a church. It seemed suspicious. But I knew deep down Seth was a cool guy and didn't have any bad intentions or anything against me, so I finally agreed to go with him and check it out.

So we went to a meeting, and about 10 people were hanging around, singing songs with their heads bowed while a guy played guitar. Cameron could see I looked lost and out of place, so he handed me a paper with lyrics on it. I soon figured out everyone was singing about how much they loved God and how much he loved them. At first I thought this was really strange, but as I sat there and read lyric after lyric, something inside me began to change. I started to feel myself soften. My emotions began swirling around somewhere inside. Then without warning I found myself kneeling down with my face on the floor. It happened so fast I felt kind of out of control, which scared me. I started crying like crazy—just weeping—and I couldn't comprehend what was happening to me.

People began to surround me and gently speak to me. They told me God has a purpose for my life and loves me. There it was: the concept I'd been grappling with for so long. I couldn't believe this was all just coincidence. Maybe there was a purpose for me and a reason I hadn't died yet.

Then all at once I felt what I can now only describe as the presence of God come upon me. My body felt weightless and as if I was floating on a cloud of pure love. It blew my mind because I had no doubt it was God. The feeling of love had never so suddenly overwhelmed me.

I left there knowing something inside of me had dramatically changed. I'd found the desire to live.

This new feeling of hope was so different from anything I'd felt in my life—I wanted to continue exploring what it meant for me. I started attending a local church where I learned more about God and began to find reasons for living other than myself.

One weekend I volunteered to help out at a street fair the church sponsored each winter. I was working a booth when I met some people who were going to Russia to help out in some orphanages there. I had no idea people just went to other countries and helped people like that! It amazed and intrigued me. Before long I couldn't shake the urge to join them.

I ended up raising support and eventually went to Russia where I quickly fell in love with the orphans who'd been abandoned, many just because they weren't what their culture deemed "perfect." The kids were perceived as damaged goods—not worthy of raising. That just blew my mind.

I still find it remarkable I lived so many years not understanding how life could be worth living. I'm alive only because God drew me to himself, and my dream of dying is dead. Before, I wanted to die, yet I had no assurance there'd be anything after death. Now I no longer have a desire to die, but I'm assured that even when this body gives out, I'll never truly die. "Alive, I'm Christ's messenger; dead, I'm his bounty. Life versus even more life! I can't lose." (Philippians 1:21, *The Message*)

For now I'm just taking one day at a time and seeking what God wants me to do. I'm just living at his disposal and hoping to be as useful as possible. One thing's for sure: Life is no longer pointless and boring.

From time to time I run into people I knew in high school, and I tell them about my life now. They generally remember me as a nonengaged, reclusive person, so they're shocked to see how I've changed. They usually say

they see me as a completely different person than I was in high school.

That's an understatement!

Ace Armstrong

BACK ON THE RIGHT TRACK

> *"Get rid of all bitterness, rage, anger, harsh words, and slander, as well as all types of malicious behavior. Instead, be kind to each other, tenderhearted, forgiving one another, just as God through Christ has forgiven you."*

—Ephesians 4:31-32, NLT

My mother is a drug addict and has been for as long as I can remember.

I lived mostly with my grandparents while my mom wandered in and out of my life. My mom said she wanted to be there for me and be the mother little girls are supposed to have, but because of her serious drug addiction, I could never really rely on her for anything.

My father was in the picture a little but had his own problems and family to deal with, so mainly it was just my grandparents, me, and sometimes my mom.

I grew up struggling with feelings of shame and resentment and was always afraid people would find out about Mom. I can remember a time when she showed up wasted at teacher conferences; I was so humiliated I just wanted to make her go away and stay out of my life.

Then during the summer before seventh grade I went to a camp with my youth group. I learned a lot about myself, and I also made the decision to give my life to God. But living as Christ would have me live wasn't easy when it came to my mother. She didn't live with us then, but when she was around, I spent most of our time together fussing at her or preaching about what not to do. I'd become the responsible one my family could always count on, as my mother'd had problems since her early teens.

At the end of eighth grade my mom called me while I was at a friend's house. She told me she'd gone into liver failure and doctors didn't expect her to live six months. I broke down when I realized she could soon be gone from my life. I went home, and we just cried together. That was when we both finally agreed to forgive each other. She also promised me she'd never do drugs again. I was somewhat skeptical because I'd heard it all before, but I decided to go along with it and give her a chance.

Things were great for a while, but then she started going off with friends again and staying gone for days, even weeks, at a time. Then all of a sudden, things came to a screeching halt.

We're still not sure what caused it, but my mother was involved in a near-fatal car crash. She'd been in the back seat sleeping. While the driver walked away with hardly a scratch, my mother got a deep gash in her head requiring 17 stitches, a dislocated shoulder, a broken back, and several chipped bones in her neck. We didn't know if she'd live, much less walk again.

When I saw my mom for the first time after the accident, I just felt like screaming. I was sick of her choices that constantly made her less and less available to be a mom. But what got to me most was she behaved just like she did on drugs. Even though I knew she'd been highly sedated because of her extensive injuries, and I was aware that this time it wasn't her choice, something inside me just snapped every time I got near her. I just couldn't stand being around her. I'd get into huge arguments with her over petty things and practically bite her head off. I knew what I was doing was wrong, but I just couldn't seem to stop myself.

Soon after Mom came home, I left for camp, and the whole time I was plagued by thoughts of how I'd behaved toward my mom. I couldn't figure out how to let go of my resentment and hatred—and it was eating me up inside. I finally shared my story with my youth group for the first time, and I asked them to pray I could somehow overcome those feelings.

I learned a lot of things that week from many great people, but when I came home, none of it seemed to take effect. My mother even became a Christian in the midst of her troubles, yet I still snapped and yelled and treated her like dirt. I justified my actions by telling myself I had a right to be mad and she deserved my punishment. But I began to hate myself and was becoming more and more miserable.

Finally I realized I had to stop what I was doing. I knew my actions were hurting my mother's newfound relationship with God. I also recognized I was just as much responsible for keeping my mom and me apart as she was—and it was time to try to meet her halfway. That's when I broke down and found myself on my knees. I begged God to help me get rid of the resentment I was holding against my mom and to forgive me for what I'd done. I also asked God to help my mom forgive me as well. I'd said some incredibly hurtful things to her.

Since that day we've been working things out and getting things back on the right track. I can't say it's not hard, or that I don't have to bite my tongue sometimes

when I'm around her, because it is, and I do. But I know I have God to help me and give me patience. With God as the center point of our relationship, forgiveness has been possible, hearts and habits have changed, and healing has taken place.

I asked God to help break a lifetime of resentment and find a way to forgiveness.

He responded. He gave me back my sense of peace, but more important, he gave me back my mom.

Kristin Greene

OPENING TO LOVE

*"I refresh the humble and give new courage
to those with repentant hearts."*

—Isaiah 57:15, NLT

I'm not sure why we did it. Even when I think about it now, I still can't begin to figure out what was going on in my head at that point in time.

Once we got caught, a pair of security guards brought us to a room full of TVs showing all the cameras in the store. Then they made my friend and me call our parents.

Nothing can break your heart the way breaking your mother's heart does. It hurt me to see her hurt and know she was disappointed in me. But as much as that night should've taught me a lesson, it didn't. I never shoplifted again, but I did get caught up in potentially worse things: drugs and alcohol.

I started drinking at parties when I was almost 17. I didn't think it too big a deal; I mean, who doesn't drink? But I took it to the extreme: I'd get drunk on school nights because I loved the buzz I got from feeling free and out of control. Nothing could hurt me when I was under the

influence of alcohol, and I liked being able to escape reality, even if it was just temporary.

This behavior continued throughout my first year at college. I stayed in what's known as the "party" dorm, and that's where my experience with drugs began. I didn't do or try any "hard drugs," just marijuana, and it seemed everyone at school smoked it as if it were water and vital for survival.

I tried pot at one of our first major parties and found the high unlike any other—even *better* than being drunk. My use of marijuana continued on and off throughout the first semester until the unthinkable happened.

I returned to my dorm room, extremely intoxicated, having been to a bar. I decided to smoke a joint with a friend *IN* my room...a major rule breaker. I'd like to say I was so drunk I wasn't thinking right, but that's no excuse. I was confronted about it by our house president, and although they weren't 100 percent sure it was me, I admitted to it. I believe that was my turning point.

The house committee took a week to try to figure out whether they should kick me out of the dorm. During that week I had a lot of time to think and reflect. Waiting brought new feelings and a new outlook. I wanted to stay at the college so badly (partying aside) because for the first time I felt as if I belonged, and I didn't want to lose that.

I prayed (for the first time in a very long time) for God to let me stay. After a few nights of this I began to feel selfish, so I started praying and apologizing for what I'd done. I apologized to everyone I'd hurt in the process. By the end of the week I just prayed. Prayed and prayed and prayed. I prayed for anything and everything, even the birth of a new day—and if you knew me then, you would've thought this quite unusual.

Nonetheless, I was expelled altogether. I cried and cried, but for the first time I wasn't mad at God or anyone else—I was mad at myself. On the last night I was there I decided to go on a walk around campus by myself to think. I was completely sober and drug-free, and I came to a great realization: I needed a relationship with God more than ever. And I not only *needed* a relationship with him—I *wanted* one.

If you knew me at that time, you'd understand just how hard it was for me to admit that. But I was tired of the path I was traveling; I wanted to love myself, but I felt I needed God to love me first. I had a few things to take care of, so I hurried back to the dorm before it got too late.

I hugged, apologized to, and cried with my roommate, and then I wrote a letter. The letter was about my "epiphany" with advice not to make the same mistake I did. I told my roommate to make copies and put them up around the campus. Then I went upstairs and apologized to the house president. After that I called my mom just to tell her I love her.

Finally, at the end of the night I prayed before going to sleep; I prayed for everything in my life. I even prayed for the bad experiences to continue helping me become who I was becoming through this experience. I felt very calm and peaceful going to sleep that night.

It's almost a year later, and much has changed: I'm now going to church, praying, and even attending a religious university to keep me connected to God. I have a better social life with the best of friends who don't judge me based on my past. I have a great relationship with my family, a job, good grades, and a loving boyfriend, and things couldn't be any better.

But most important, I have a relationship with God, and I know he's forgiven me and loves me. And in turn I've learned to love myself. I've realized the surest way to find God is not to make him a private possession, a problem solver, or an instant consolation in time of need, but to open yourself to love.

Like the apostle John said: "God is love, and all who live in love live in God, and God lives in them" (1 John 4:16, NLT).

I will never forget the night most people would refer to as the worst night of my life. I call it a miracle.

Ashley Kinden

NEVER ALONE

> *"So do not fear, for I am with you; do not be dismayed, for I am your God. I will strengthen you and help you."*

—Isaiah 41:10

"Why can't I talk to people, God? I'm sick of being alone!"

I slumped against the wall, crying for the fifth week in a row. *What's youth "group" when you're all by yourself?* I wondered. I hurt so much I wanted to kick the wall. All around me were happy teens talking and laughing about things like music and school. But I wasn't. As far back as I could remember, I'd never fit into their world.

Being shy wasn't easy or fun. People scared me. Fear controlled my life, and I felt helpless to do anything about it. *God, are you there? Do you hear me anymore? I'm 16, and I want some friends...I want to be normal!* I kept praying, but God's answer wasn't showing up. I became lonelier and more depressed each week, thinking, *I'll never get out of this black hole...will I?*

One night my youth pastor asked me if I was okay. With a laugh I said, "I don't know anymore."

HE IS A GOD OF TRANSFORMATION

At the same time I was thinking, *I'm so crazy I don't even know if I'm okay or not.*

Pastor Ted asked, "Why don't you talk to people, Laura?"

I sat silently, looking at the carpet. "I...it's like...I just can't. I can't start conversations. I don't know how." Fear paralyzed me when I saw people, scared they would reject me. *Laura, you have a sick mind!* I thought. *What are these kids gonna do? Walk away when you open your mouth?* But there was still the issue of just what do you say to people. I didn't know what to ask questions about.

"Laura," Ted began, "next week I want you to go up to someone and compliment that person. Say you like her outfit. Ask her where she got her shoes."

So it's supposed to be that easy? You just walk up to someone and start talking? I didn't think so.

Ted continued, "You've memorized Bible verses since you were a little girl. Now you're gonna have to put them to work. I want you to step out on the water in faith and walk. Either you *can* do all things through Christ...or God's a liar."

I gulped. It wasn't that I thought God was a liar...I just had the "why me?" syndrome. *If you really are listening, God, then please tell me* why *I've been silent for so long and* why *I feel so alone and depressed.*

Just then Ted's words broke through my thoughts. "I think you need an extreme makeover. You need to make some major changes in your life. I know you can do this."

Lying in bed that night, I let my mind replay the conversation. My whisper bounced off the ceiling. "I do want to talk. I *have* to talk. *I need friends!*"

I woke up the next morning with a desire to change. An extreme makeover sounded good to me. Hair, clothes, room, attitude, wardrobe, interests—I wanted them all to change.

The next Tuesday night I took the initiative, and while reciting *I can do all things through Christ who gives me strength,* I breathed deeply and walked over to a girl who was sitting by herself.

"Hi! What's up?" I asked.

With those three words God was beginning to heal my heart and stop the fear that controlled my life.

In the following months I talked more and made a few friends. But I wasn't reading my Bible much or seeking God. I made up lots of excuses for ignoring God, such as, *I'm just trying to deal with my life right now.*

But one week at summer camp can change everything. And it did. I heard messages on loneliness for the first time ever. My heart was hurting. Shyness, depression, and loneliness messed up my mind so much. Being in denial doesn't help people heal; it just stuffs the pain. "I desperately need to get over this, God!" I prayed with tears trickling down my cheeks.

One morning our camp speaker asked everyone who felt alone to stand up. I couldn't jump up fast enough. After that meeting the girls in my cabin showered me with love, and I saw for the first time people cared...even about me. That helped calm my fears and my preconceptions that people would reject me if I showed them the real me.

Later that week in chapel I was still feeling vulnerable and found myself crying again. *I can't run anymore, God. I have to learn to trust you! I need to trust that you won't let people reject me if I open up to them.*

"If you're hurting and in need of God's help, come on down to the altar and pray," our speaker suddenly said, jolting me away from my thoughts.

I sat there, realizing if I stayed silent, nothing would change. *I want to break free from my fears, God, but I'm so afraid to be vulnerable.*

A statement made by our camp speaker earlier in the week really touched me. He said sometimes Christians look perfect because they hold it all inside. It made me realize, especially after being at camp and hearing other people share about their personal issues, that some of my new friends felt the same way. And it also showed me their lives weren't perfect, either.

At that point I knew I needed to start asking God for help instead of always asking why he made me like this. Freedom was right in front of me, and I wanted out from under this agony more than ever.

The night before we left camp, I sat down with my leader, Kelly, and finally poured out to her all that was bothering me. Kelly looked at me with such compassion after hearing me out. With tears in her eyes she said, "I feel you're ready to let go of your fears. Can you do it?"

I was as ready as I'd ever been, so I silently prayed, *God, give me strength...I'm giving all my fears and hopes to you now.* It was so hard to release control and hand it over to God, but as soon as I said that prayer, my heart felt lighter than it had in years.

Looking back I recall there wasn't one day that week at camp when I walked alone. Angelina held me. Val and Paola hugged me. Tressa talked to me. Kelly understood.

God helped me break free and become someone who could take the initiative to communicate with others. And as I moved forward in faith, I believed God would help me, and I learned I can face risking personal rejection because Jesus holds me up. He gives me courage to talk. And he stops the fear.

One night after camp I actually jumped at the chance to tell a huge crowd of people at our church's volleyball league how God had changed my heart at camp. Each week they set up a sound system for speakers to use and discuss faith. There was no way in the world I would've done that before turning my fears over to God. I know only by God's grace alone could I stand before a hundred teens and speak. Trembling as I was, I'd acquired an indescribable happiness since I released everything to God. I wanted to tell others about it because the change was just so remarkable.

Ever since that summer I've had faithful friends surrounding me. They've helped me embrace God's love and trust him to rescue me from shyness, loneliness, and depression.

That summer God gave me a chance to turn my life around, and I took it. It required me to shut the door of my past, turn the key, and step out in faith.

I found true freedom.

Laura Farrar

HE IS A GOD OF TRANSFORMATION

RUNNING TOWARD MY FEARS

"But the Lord has promised to fight on our side and to rescue our children from those strong and violent enemies. He will make those cruel people dine on their own flesh and get drunk from drinking their own blood. Then everyone will know that the Lord is our Savior."

—Isaiah 49:25-26, CEV

Playing on the monkey bars was one of my favorite things to do when I was four. I lived in a small town, and life was laid-back and easy. My parents allowed me in the neighborhood by myself because in their minds, they had nothing to fear.

But it wasn't long before I found out there was more to fear than they could ever imagine.

He was a neighbor and familiar to me, so when he approached me as I swung from ring to ring, my instinct wasn't to run but to find out what he wanted. He pulled out a pocketknife and threatened that if I didn't come with him and do exactly what he asked, he'd hurt me and my family, too.

Most of the ensuing abuses took place at his nearby apartment where he lived with a few members of the cult he was in. I found out he meant what he said when one day he took me to see a cat he'd killed. Apparently slaughtering neighborhood pets was one of his favorite pastimes, among even more horrific things. I was haunted for years by what he did to me.

It wasn't long after he sexually abused me and threatened to destroy me and my family that he drew me into strange ceremonies—satanic rituals—over the course of the next two years.

I was so confused and scared for my life I felt I had no choice but to do what he demanded.

I remember having constant bladder infections and going to the doctor for them, but I was never thoroughly examined because I guess sexual abuse just wasn't suspected for some reason. I also used to throw up very easily, and the doctors said I had a "nervous stomach." I'd hoped somehow my mom would put my symptoms and strange behavior together and figure it all out, but the way I finally escaped the torture of my neighbor and his cult was when my family moved to a town about 20 minutes away. I would've preferred to move halfway around the world, but just getting away from there brought some relief—at least temporarily.

My family began attending a church near our new home. The pastor there had a couple of sons in their teens. I was about seven when they began sexually abusing me, and again I was caught up in a cycle of abuse and secrecy.

I soon began suffering from insomnia. I'd have terrible nightmares that freaked me out so badly I couldn't get back to sleep. Then I started to notice at church during communion I would do just about anything to get out of

the sanctuary. The concept of drinking Christ's blood and eating his body just threw me into a state of panic. The memories of cult members drinking human blood terrorized me. I'd often get so nauseous during communion I'd throw up.

By my junior year in high school it became obvious I had no interest in dating. I had guy friends, but when it came to displaying any kind of affection, even kissing, I'd freak. I'd acquired an aversion to men, and I didn't want anything to do with a romantic relationship.

When a friend asked me to the senior prom, I figured I could handle that. But somehow we ended up in his car, and he made a move on me and totally freaked me out. That triggered memories of the horrors of my childhood, and after that night my mind began reliving the terror and abuses all over again.

Shortly after the prom I began having terrible pain in my reproductive organs. It got so bad I was bedridden for days, just crumpled up in pain. Some days it was so unbearable I couldn't even walk. It felt as if my insides were being shredded.

I'd just begun attending a Christian college and was living with a wonderful family near my school. As my condition got progressively worse, the parents of this family saw the pain I was in, and they began trying to care for me. In that process my childhood secrets were finally revealed—and to make a long story short, that spurred an investigation with the police back in the town where the satanic ritual abuse had taken place.

Meanwhile, I began seeing a doctor about my abdominal pain. After performing various tests, my doctor could only guess at what was going on. He suspected I had endometriosis, a scarring phenomenon that causes pain and even infertility problems. Until I could be scheduled for exploratory surgery, he prescribed painkillers, which I gradually took in higher and higher doses to try and ease the pain. But no matter how many I took—eventually 16 pills a day—I could never get relief. Obviously all those painkillers lowered my ability to function, which wasn't good since I was taking 23 units in school and holding down a job. All this, along with the stress of the investigation, finally put me over the edge.

To put it mildly, I was a mess.

I looked forward to the relief I expected the surgery to provide, but when the doctors examined my insides, they said everything looked fine and concluded nothing was wrong with me. I was in the worst pain of my life, and I knew, even if no one else did, I wasn't making it up.

I began grasping for reasons why it felt as if my insides were being torn away when the doctors couldn't find anything wrong. In desperation I e-mailed people at several different Christian Web sites who had experience dealing with satanic ritual abuse. I learned abdominal pain isn't uncommon among women who've been through SRA. Two people e-mailed back and said they'd heard about a Christian ministry that might be able to help me. I was like, "Yeah, right. I can hardly function, I'm nearly broke, and I'm going to get myself across the country to this ministry?"

I had also e-mailed some Christians who'd mentored me and let them know what was going on. Strangely enough, I received an e-mail back from a woman who said she had a book she wanted to share with me from the same ministry I'd just been told about. She'd gone there to seek the possible spiritual roots of a disease she was struggling with. *Is God directing me to this place?* I wondered.

By the time the fourth person, who didn't know the others, referred me to the same ministry, I decided maybe I should look into it even though I didn't have the resources to get there.

The next thing that happened gave me all the confirmation I needed. The woman who'd been there and came back healed offered to pay all of my expenses so I could get help.

Within days I was heading across the country!

One of the first sessions at the ministry was a teaching about God the Father's love. I'd been over and over this concept so many times I wondered if I was just going to rehash something I'd already learned. There was an invitation to come up front if you wanted extra help in this area. So I asked God if I even needed to hear this message or what I should do. I heard him tell me, "Go up."

"Go up? I thought I already dealt with all this," I pleaded as I began to inch my way up the aisle toward the front of the room. As I did, I heard God say that while I did deal with issues between me and my earthly father, I hadn't fully allowed God to step in as my Father.

"Well, duh," I responded as a list of reasons ran through my head.

As all this was being communicated to me, I was suddenly given a picture in my mind. It was a memory of when the abusive, Satan-worshiping neighbor held a knife to my throat as he threatened my life. I clearly saw God's hand come between the knife and my throat—and God's hand was being cut up. God said to me, "That is where you're wrong; it's only by my hand that you are even alive."

I immediately dropped to my knees in the aisle and began weeping. It was such a turning point in my heart. I realized I'd blamed God without a thought of the possibility he'd actually intervened at times when I was in danger.

The experience opened my heart and helped me receive so much more out of the week at the ministry. I was able to ask God about specific times I felt abandoned. He showed me vision after vision of where he'd been and how his heart had broken for me. The best thing from those visions was that they took the power Satan had over the memories and allowed me to understand God's heart in it all.

During one of the sessions later that week I heard God tell me that my self-hatred—which had resulted from the abuse—was the cause of the pain I'd been experiencing. My self-loathing was so deep within my being that my organs had actually turned on themselves. Then he explained I needed to deal with my self-hatred. I wasn't sure how I was going to do that, but God's plan was only just beginning to unfold.

On another day that week I was in my room taking a nap, and I had a dream. I was in an airport, and a guy came up to me. He seemed really confused but asked me if I had a dollar. I was like, "Yeah, why?" The man in my dream responded, "I wonder if you'd like to buy one of these?" He opened up a briefcase full of avocados. In my dream I was thinking, *This is so bizarre. He seems confused; I'm confused. Maybe I should buy one.*

So I pulled out a dollar and went to hand it to him, and the man said, "No. I think I'm supposed to give it to you as a gift." As he went to hand it to me, I woke up.

I've always had a severe allergy to avocados. If I accidentally ate avocado (I'd never do it on purpose), I'd

go into anaphylactic shock and could die. It was that bad. Even if I touched avocado, I'd break out in a rash. I hadn't even thought about my allergy going into my week at the ministry because I had bigger issues on my mind.

So when I first woke up, I didn't think anything of the dream or whether it had any meaning. I lay on the bed, and I began to hear gurgling in my throat. It kept up for a while, and I decided that if I could just go back to sleep, it'd be gone when I woke up. I wrestled around trying to fall back asleep but couldn't. Finally, I prayed, "God, help me fall back asleep." Then I heard God say, "No, I'm doing something. I just extended your throat and your airways."

I began to wonder if I was crazy when I heard God say, "I just healed your allergy. Your dream represented two things: Your need for healing and your fears."

God continued by saying, "I wanted to see if you were willing to invest in your healing, and when I saw that you were willing to invest in it, I gave you this gift."

My first reaction was somewhat ungrateful; I kind of whined back at him, "I really don't care if I ever eat avocados again. I'd have rather been cured of this pain I've been suffering from."

Then I heard God promise, "I'm going to do it all, but I need to do it in my timing and in my own way. But this is a deposit on your healing. This will be a tangible sign to you: When you eat avocados without a reaction, you'll be reminded that I'll finish healing you. But before I can, you need to learn to run toward your fears."

*Run toward my fears...run toward my fears...*I pondered this over and over, wondering just how to do that. As I carefully considered the things that had terrified me throughout my life, I began to challenge them one by one, head-on.

I began by calling my friend, asking if she'd make her avocado salad for dinner when I got back. She said she was already planning on making it but was going to make one for me without the avocado as usual. I told her to make it all the same because I'd be eating it.

When I sat down to dinner with the family upon my return, they were all nervous and watched as I took my first few bites. They were well aware I could go into shock. But I had no reaction—and I've never had a reaction since. I eat avocado all the time now.

As I worked on "running toward my fears" and trusting God to protect me, I slowly sensed myself healing. I began doing things such as lighting candles, which had always freaked me out, possibly because the room where the ritual ceremonies took place was always candlelit.

For years I had an aversion to knives and a hard time touching a knife even to cook. But I began holding and using knives, and eventually the bondage to fear of knives began to fall away.

As I continued to delve into God's Word and accept truth about what God wanted for me, I finally found a way to forgive myself and the people who'd wronged me. My self-hatred was being replaced with the knowledge that I was loved as a child of God. Eventually, the pain in my abdomen began to subside until it one day it was simply gone.

It has never returned.

One thing God made clear is that as uncomfortable as it can be for me, he wouldn't allow me to pass up an opportunity to share my story. Although writing this was

one more fear I had to face, God assured me he'd give me the wisdom and discernment to tell about the great transformation he worked in me.

Sharing about God's amazing works of healing, miracles in my life, and love has become easier and brought me a lot of joy.

When I tell about what God has done, his glory and the hope he offers each of us shine through the undeniable evidence: Evidence of how God made this broken and hurting young girl—who'd been torn apart by fear and self-hatred—into a whole, healthy, and happy young woman who now lives only to serve God.

Anonymous

THE CRASH

> *"First pride, then the crash—the bigger the ego, the harder the fall."*
>
> —Proverbs 16:18, *The Message*

It was my first time leading a Bible study. Was I nervous or scared? No way! I was in charge and had total confidence I'd do a great job. (Let's call that mistake #1.)

I'd agreed to help friends from church lead a college-age youth group. Many of the students in the group weren't much younger than I was, but I think it's safe to say most of them were much closer to God than I was.

The leader had asked me to lead on a night he'd be gone. I devoted myself to preparing for the study but didn't spend much time praying and asking God to help me. (Let's call that mistake #2.)

When I left work the afternoon of the study, I found my car blocked by several other cars. I searched for the drivers and patiently waited while they moved their cars. I breathed a sigh of relief as I got into mine and turned the key. Nothing happened. I heard a few clicks but not much else. Being the mechanical wizard I am, I quickly

determined I'd left my lights on—the battery was very, very dead.

Instead of being discouraged or frustrated, I was excited. I assumed the enemy was attacking me. I thought Satan felt so threatened by my brilliant Bible study that he was trying to stop me from getting there.

I sailed back into work with a huge grin on my face and found someone to jump-start my car. I generously praised myself for handling my car problems in a way that showed great spiritual maturity. (Let's call that mistake #3.)

On the way to the study I passed a stalled car and offered the stranded driver a ride. I chatted about myself nonstop on the way to her home. I was immune to the strange look she gave me as she rushed to get out of the car. I was so busy patting myself on the back for my good deed I barely noticed that when she greeted her husband, she pointed at my car and waved her finger in a circle around her ear. The fact that she thought I was crazy obviously meant she wasn't as in touch with God as I was.

I arrived at the church and began making sure everything was perfectly in order for my brilliant study. I remember being a little annoyed because the students didn't seem to be in a big hurry to settle down and get quiet for the enlightenment I was about to bless them with. I asked God to forgive them and forged ahead.

We usually started our studies with a time of worship led by Brian. Since Brian wasn't there, I'd copied some song lyrics and planned to spend a few minutes listening to the song before discussing the beauty of the lyrics. (Did I mention the song was in Spanish? Let's call that mistake #4.) Imagine my indignation when one of the college students got out his guitar and told me Brian had asked *him* to lead worship. Instead of being thankful Brian

had planned ahead and made arrangements for worship, I was angry. I was angry my great idea wasn't going to be used, and I was angry Brian had taken the liberty of arranging a part of MY study. How dare he!

I'm afraid my worship that night wasn't very God-honoring. (It's tough to sing through clenched teeth.) I consoled myself with the thought that my time to shine was close at hand. I started the study by bragging about the good deed I'd done and about how well I'd handled the "extreme spiritual attack." I focused the study on Galatians 6:7: "Do not be deceived: God cannot be mocked. A man reaps what he sows."

Although it's not pertinent to this story, I need to confess I pronounced *sow* wrong through the entire study—I referenced female pigs instead of planting seeds. (Let's call that mistake #5.)

I didn't ask questions or try to generate a discussion as I spoke. The students in the group responded politely, but I don't think any of them saw burning bushes or chariots of fire. I took advantage of my captive audience to share a recital of the many things that made me wonderful. When it ended, I basked in the praise I received from a few kids and tried to ignore the ones who were beating a hasty retreat. I wafted to my car enveloped in a cloud of self-praise. I paused occasionally to give thanks to God, but most of my praise was for me. (Let's call those mistakes 6-10.)

As I drove home, I was at a stop sign when warmth suddenly filled the car. I felt God's intimate presence in a way I'd never felt it before. I very clearly heard him ask in the depths of my soul, "Whom were you trying to glorify? You or me?"

In an instant the ugliness of my attitude and behavior became clear. The weight of God's disappointment was

more than I could bear. He showed me that my obsession with bringing glory and attention to myself instead of God was not just sinful but a betrayal of his love. I felt an overwhelming mixture of shame, sadness, and shock at how self-centered I'd been. I sobbed as I asked God to forgive me and help me never sink to that level of prideful self-worship again.

God's response came clearly and gently. He reminded me it's his job to teach, not mine. God shared that he couldn't work through me to teach and encourage others until I learned to submit to him and die to myself. In the midst of my despair God encouraged me with Jeremiah 29:11: "'For I know the plans I have for you,' says the Lord. 'They are plans for good and not for disaster, to give you a future and a hope'" (NLT).

I clung to the hope God offered and asked him not to let me lead another Bible study until I could lead in a way honoring to him.

Three long years passed before I led another study. During that time God showed me I had much to learn. He taught me many things and lovingly changed my heart. God had to break my pride and change me in dramatic ways before he could allow me to lead again.

The sin of pride is still a constant battle for me, but the words God spoke to me after that first Bible study have altered my approach to life. I now give each day to God before I get out of bed. I continually ask God to help me die to myself so I can bring honor and glory to him.

Living a life focused on God and not on myself isn't always easy, but God is faithful to give me the strength I need to submit to him in all things, and he forgives me when I don't.

(Let's call that right thing #1.)

Pamela Reilly

HE IS A GOD OF RECOVERY AND RESTORATION.

"He will renew your life and sustain you."
—Ruth 4:15

RECLAIMED

"And the God of all grace, who called you to his eternal glory in Christ, after you have suffered a little while, will himself restore you and make you strong, firm and steadfast."

—1 Peter 5:10

"You drink first," I said. "No, you," my friend Michael replied.

So I took a drink. I remember it burning and tasting awful, but I wasn't going to let on I didn't like it. I passed the bottle to Michael, and we continued doing this until it was all gone. When I stood up, the whole world started spinning. We staggered back into my house and somehow managed not to get caught by my parents.

That night during my freshman year of high school was the beginning of what almost destroyed my life.

I was born to two wonderful parents. My dad was so excited to have a son. He'd never known his dad, and he wanted to be the best dad he possibly could. He was.

Dad was also very athletic and always encouraged me in sports. At the start of my eighth-grade year, I had

a growth explosion, so I chose to devote my sports career to football. My dad would practice with me in the back-yard until it was too dark to see. I was viewed as one of the star players on the team.

My parents also made sure I was in church every Sunday. My mother would often talk to me about the Bible stories I learned. I especially loved David and Goliath. I told my mother one day, "I'm going to be like David. I'll never be a bully like Goliath." She smiled and said, "I know God is going to do something big with your life one day, Eric. You just remember what you learn and apply it to your life, and he'll take care of you."

The summer when I was nine years old, I began asking a lot of questions about God. So one afternoon our preacher came over to the house. We sat out on the front porch, and after a lot of discussion he asked me if I wanted to become a Christian. "All you have to do is ask Jesus to come into your heart and forgive you for your sins. Is that what you want to do?"

"Yes!" I said.

So I prayed right there on my front porch and really believed. A couple of Sundays later I was baptized.

After church sometimes I was invited to play at friends' houses. One day as I was walking down the road with a friend from church, he looked down and saw a six-pack ring of Budweiser with one beer left in it. He quickly grabbed it and stuffed it in his jacket. He wanted to drink it and said I was a sissy if I didn't at least try it, so I did. I hated it and actually spit it out. He laughed at me, so I took another drink. I wish that had been the last drink I ever took.

When I got to the eighth grade, I started not want-ing to go to church because I wanted to sleep in. Then at school I began to get a reputation as a tough guy. I started sneaking cigarettes out of the teachers' lounge between classes and with a friend of mine, Dennis, started smoking after school behind his house and in a wooded lot beside my house.

In the ninth grade it came time to have our annual homecoming parade, and I wanted to help build the float. We'd heard someone was going to buy booze for anyone who wanted it. All we had to do was give him a few extra dollars. Sure enough, a guy came up and asked us if we wanted anything from the liquor store. That was the night my friend Michael and I ended up with a pint of Jim Beam whiskey and the first time I truly got drunk.

As time went by, I got better and better at football. I made varsity as a freshman and started as a 10th grader. I was running with the big dogs now. I had the respect of my teammates as a good player and of my church as a good boy. What people didn't know was I'd acquired a taste for alcohol.

Soon Travis, an older star player on the team, became a good friend. I started hanging out with the older guys through him. I turned 16, and Travis' family gave me a key to their lake property and told me I could do what I wanted there but not to let things get out of hand.

Having access to a place like that, I quickly became known for being a wild partier with a filthy mouth. Every weekend I could, I would host a big party at the lake. Several carloads of people would come up, and we'd get someone to buy alcohol for us. I even got the nerve to buy it a few times. I guess because of my size, the clerks didn't think I was underage, or they just didn't care. I became the life of the party.

One night at a party in town I got so drunk I passed out. When I didn't come home, my parents started calling

people. My mom was a nervous wreck and automatically thought the worst. "He's been in an accident—I just know it!" she said to my dad. Some friends had driven me to my house and left me passed out in my truck. They hadn't parked it where I normally parked, and no one could see it from any window in our house, so my parents didn't know I was there. They finally talked to a guy who'd carried me home, and my mom came out and woke me up. I cussed at her, and she slapped me. My dad is a hard worker and physically imposing. He grabbed me, and we got into a scuffle. I remember the hurt in his eyes when I could see he really didn't know what to do.

My football coach told me he'd heard some bad rumors about me and if he heard them again, he'd tell my parents. I looked him straight in the face and lied to him. Lying was no longer hard for me. I just told people what I thought they wanted to hear.

The summer between my sophomore and junior year I tried to get in shape for the upcoming season. My dad told me he was very proud of me and how hard I was working. People around town really expected us to win the state championship game and told me how they were counting on me.

The first game of the season was the highlight of my football career. I made several sacks and was named county player of the week. My dad was so proud of me, and the community rallied around our team. Instead of focusing on staying in shape I went on a weekend drinking spree after that game to celebrate what'd happened. The following Monday I did terribly in practice, and I knew why. I was dragging from the lack of sleep and was hung over from a weekend of partying. Coach knew something was up, and he let me know that just because I'd shined in the first game didn't mean he wouldn't let me ride the bench the rest of the season.

My drinking continued. I began to lose interest in working out and staying in shape—I just wanted to have fun. Our homecoming game was in the middle of the season, and there was another float to build, so I went with another friend of mine. We'd been drinking heavily, and when we were backing up, we smashed into a car, but the guy driving sped off.

"Go back!" I said. "Everyone saw us hit the car! We're going to go to jail!"

The driver said the car we hit belonged to the mayor, who also served as probation officer. I thought football was finished for me for good. In spite of that I talked the driver into going back and hoping for the best.

When we got back to the parking lot, a huge crowd was gathered around the car, and the mayor was standing there, looking at the damage. He waved everyone off, came up to the car door, looked in at us, and said, "Boys, that was a stupid thing to do. You've been drinking, haven't you?"

"Yes, sir, and we're sorry! Please let us just pay you for the damage and go home!" I begged.

"Well, you boys make 25 tackles tomorrow night, and I'll forget about this," he said with a smile on his face. I couldn't believe it. The highest town official had just busted us...and let us go.

We left there thinking we were invincible. I look back now and wish I had been taught a lesson because from that point my life really began to spiral downward.

I partied every Thursday night and on the weekends for the rest of the football season. I was starting but not getting as much playing time. I made stupid mistakes that cost us big-time in some games. Several times Coach

pulled me out of the game for an entire quarter because I was so out of shape and couldn't keep up. The season ended during the third round of the state playoffs, and everyone knew something was wrong but couldn't believe I was really drinking that much.

After the football season tragedy struck. A close friend of mine committed suicide. Shane was a good guy. He never drank and partied, and I'd always respected him for his positive attitude. He told everyone his goal was to become a Navy fighter pilot, and we all knew he could do it. He was extremely close to his family, especially his younger sister. Cheerleader tryouts came along, and his little sister made the squad. I remember him lifting her up and telling her how proud he was of her. One day as we walked out to the parking lot after school, he looked at me and told me he loved me and I'd always been a good friend. I thought that was weird and just said, "Okay, man. I'll see you tomorrow."

The next morning my mother came into my room and woke me up.

"Eric, I have some bad news to tell you," she said with tears coming down her face. "Shane died this morning."

I couldn't believe it, and I wouldn't believe it. But I went on to school, and everyone was walking around like zombies. After school a lot of the football players got together. We talked and cried. Then someone said they were going to go get a drink. I knew in my heart I wasn't honoring Shane by doing something he wouldn't do, but I went anyway.

By the time spring practice came around, everyone knew, including me, that I was getting slower and slower, and I was just so out of shape. The spring game came, and my life took another turn toward the worst.

In the fourth quarter the other team was trying to score to win the game. It was third and goal, and a friend of mine called a stunt from the line. When I crossed the line of scrimmage, someone hit me in the back, and I fell with my arm out the wrong way. I couldn't get up. When I tried, my elbow hit my wrist, and I immediately went into shock. I'd never been in so much pain. My arm was limp as a rag.

I had to have 13 pins and two plates put in my right arm just to hold it together. They grafted bone off my hip, and I had zero-percent use of my right arm from the elbow down. I went through months of rehab, but it never seemed to work. My fingers wouldn't even twitch. Finally, I was informed I could never play football again. I wanted to die right then. I'd put my whole life into football, and it was over.

During my time in the hospital only a couple of guys from the team cared enough to stop by. The coaches never did come. When they learned I couldn't play ball anymore, they wanted to avoid me. I went from a hero to a zero.

I started skipping classes and drinking during the day when I could scrape up enough money. Only one teacher encouraged me to keep up with all my work, even if I had to make it up. I remember her telling me God could do something with a young man like me. I blew off her statement because I knew I was as far from God as I could get.

My senior year was coming to a close, and I'd just barely passed. A couple of relationships with girls ended. The football team didn't do very well that season, and I felt a few people were blaming me, so I took it all person-ally and used that as an excuse to take my partying to the next level.

In the fall I signed up for a couple of college courses, but I didn't even try to do well. Then one day I noticed the fingers on my right hand had begun to move a little, and I got really excited. I told my mom, and she took me to the hospital. The doctor who treated me said God must have a special plan for me because he thought I'd never regain full use of the hand because of nerve damage. He now thought I could expect a full recovery over time.

My heart had become so hardened I couldn't see God was giving me every chance I needed to come back to him. So my wild life continued, and I stayed away from home as much as possible. I'd stay anywhere people would let me, even though I knew they didn't care about me at all.

When I saw my parents, my dad and I would get into screaming arguments because I was filled with rage. He was trying to help me, and I didn't want help. I left several times after we almost came to blows. I was basically homeless by choice. I had a home and a family who loved me, but I was too rebellious to live anywhere that required me to follow rules.

My 19th birthday rolled around, and I was in rough shape. I could feel the effects of smoking two packs of cigarettes a day and drinking practically every night. I hated myself and my life, and thoughts of suicide became more and more a part of my days.

One evening I stopped to see my mom at work, and I met a young lady named Christy. She was a year older than me and from another school, but I knew her through some acquaintances. What I didn't know was my mom had told her I needed prayer—and Christy was a total believer in Jesus Christ. She always had a smile on her face, and she showed a real interest in me—not as a boyfriend but as a person. I went to see her on different occasions. Finally, one day I asked Christy why she was

always so happy and so nice to me. I remember what she said as if it were yesterday: "Eric, I think you're special because God thinks you're special. God loves you and has a plan for your life—don't ever forget that." Then she told me she was praying for me and was always there for me if I ever needed anything. She said she'd talk to me 24/7 if I ever needed her. She gave me her phone number, and I thanked her and left. I put the number in my wallet and didn't think any more about it.

A few weeks later a "friend" of mine wanted to introduce me to a guy just called "The Knife." I'd heard this guy was bad news, but I didn't want that "friend" to leave me, too. So we went over to The Knife's house and knocked on the door. When we stepped inside, he grabbed me, pushed me against the wall, and put a .38-caliber pistol to my head. I honestly thought he was going to kill me. I could tell by the look in his eyes he was on drugs, and I smelled whiskey on his breath.

"Who are you?!" he demanded. My friend tried to get him to calm down, but The Knife didn't even seem to hear him. Suddenly, he pulled the trigger, and I heard the click of the gun dry-firing. Then he shoved me away, spun around laughing, and said, "I guess you're all right!" He pointed the gun in the air and squeezed the trigger again. This time the gun went off. I found out that when he had an uninvited guest, that's how he determined if the guest was okay or not. He'd put one bullet in the chamber and spin the cylinder—if the bullet went off, you were dead; if it didn't, you were okay. I looked up at his ceiling, and it was full of bullet holes. I was too afraid to run and too afraid to do anything, so I just sat there hoping I could get out alive. Finally, my friend made up an excuse, and we left.

I wish I could say I never went back, but I did. This guy would get my friends and me anything we wanted, and he had money to burn. I knew he was a drug dealer

HE IS A GOD OF RECOVERY AND RESTORATION

and a thief, but all that mattered to me was having another wild night.

Then I got more bad news. One of my closest friends since childhood had been coming home from a big party at college. The truck driver behind him said he saw my friend's head slumped over on the window when the car swerved off the road. The engine from his car came through the dash and hit him in the head. He lived four hours in surgery, but his brain was too damaged. My friend since elementary school, one of the toughest people I'd ever known to play football, my teammate, my partying buddy, was gone. I dove into the bottle and the darkest depression of my life...I thought.

Then more news came to me one day: Another of my close friends from high school was killed. He was attempting to rob a convenience store to get money for his drug habit, and the owner shot him seven times. My friend had a gun, and the owner acted in self-defense; however, my friend was gone.

My mind reeled with depression, and I decided I would just finally end all the pain. I came up with a plan to go to my high school football stadium and take my life. I started driving about 4 a.m. and came through my hometown at 5 a.m. *Well, this is it*, I thought. *I'll never see this place again. In just a few minutes I'll stop this miserable life I've created.*

Then something caught my eye. It was an old telephone booth. It'd always looked so out of place just sitting out there on the corner. It'd been painted road-stripe yellow—I guess so no one would run over it. It just seemed to be in the way. For a moment I thought about how stupid it looked, and then something happened. I heard a voice, not audible, but down inside my heart. I remembered what Christy had said: "If you ever need me, I'm here 24/7. You just call me if you need me." I whipped my car over into a parking place beside the phone and sat there. Desperately, I told God, "If she is really serious, then I'll get help. If she hangs up on me, I'll die. Right here. I'll just end it right here." I dug her number out of my wallet and got out of the car. I thought what I was doing was crazy. There was no way an upstanding young lady like her was going to respond very well to a drunk calling at five in the morning. I was desperate so I dropped a quarter in and dialed the number anyway.

After a couple of rings she answered. "Hello," I said, "this is Eric. What are you doing?" Now that I look back on it, how stupid was it to call someone at five and say, "What are you doing?" But she said, "Eric, I've been praying for you. Where are you? I want to come get you."

I started crying uncontrollably. She finally got from me where I was and said she was on her way. I just sat there on the corner and cried. I was so thankful I'd seen that yellow phone booth and thought about Christy. I was so glad I hadn't killed myself.

When Christy got there, she sat me down and told me Jesus had never quit loving me even though I'd rejected all I knew was right. I asked God to forgive me for my sins, and I gave him complete control of my life right then. I knew Jesus was right there with me and heard and answered me.

Tears poured out of my eyes because I was no longer miserable. I had an unexplainable peace. All the way to my parents' house I prayed, thanking God. When we got there, I told them about what'd happened to me.

It's funny how God works when you begin to live with him in your life. I began to meet people like Keith, who encouraged me to read the Bible. I hadn't read the Bible in years and wasn't sure if I could understand it. But I got one and began reading it. I was flooded with excite-

ment when I read the Bible—a love letter written directly to me. I couldn't get enough.

So many times throughout my life people told me God had a plan for me, he could use me, and I was somehow special to him. I'd given God my life as a little kid, and no matter how far I strayed, when I called him back to me, he heard me and responded with a love, a power, so big it still blows me away. He reclaimed me.

From that day on, by the power and strength of God's love, I turned things around and began to live a life worthy of that kind of love.

All those years had led to so much misery I'd never wanted to listen to anyone. But now I actually wish I could give everyone I'd blown off who told me God had plans for me the chance to say, "I told ya so."

Eric Hixon

SATISFIED

> *"But remember this—the wrong desires that come into your life aren't anything new and different. Many others have faced exactly the same problems before you. And no temptation is irresistible. You can trust God to keep the temptation from becoming so strong that you can't stand up against it, for he has promised this and will do what he says. He will show you how to escape temptation's power so that you can bear up patiently against it."*

—1 Corinthians 10:13, LB

"Get out of here, you fairy. You're such a queer."

My classmate's face carried so much disdain and disgust I figured he saw something in me or knew something about me even I didn't know. When other kids at school continued to say the same kinds of rejecting things to me, accusing me of being gay for most of my childhood, I guess on a subliminal level it sank in—and I began to take ownership of the label.

I admit while in elementary school I did notice I had more interest in boys than girls, but I honestly don't think

I ever acted in a way that would've made the kids think I was gay. And I quickly learned they seemed to think being gay was the worst possible thing a person could be.

By high school my feelings toward boys were still there, but I continued to try to push them away because I'd seen people attacked and beaten up for having homosexual tendencies.

On top of being teased and taunted over the years, I didn't feel a lot of love or get attention at home. From the time I was in elementary school my parents would often tell me I was stupid and no good. They constantly compared me with others, saying they wished I was more like this person or that person.

It's hard to say why I took the road I did—inflicting pain on myself as punishment for being less than I should've been or eliciting pleasure to escape my pain. But when I finally found relief from my constant inner struggles, I became addicted to the feeling. It goes by the name of Ecstasy, and it was my first experience with what I can only describe as euphoria.

I was 18 years old and out of high school when two lesbian friends of mine took me out, and we ended up at a gay club. I loved the energy of the people there, and eventually, I became a regular within that club scene. It was then I first tried Ecstasy. It gave me so much energy that when a club would close at 5 a.m. and another would open at 6 a.m., I had the ability to keep on partying. This brought me a lot of attention and made me feel popular. I still continued to deny I was interested in guys, but that didn't stop gay guys from pressuring me to be with them. They were constantly pushing me just to come out and admit I was gay.

Finally, one night when I was all buzzed up on Ecstasy, I gave in to a guy. My first homosexual experience honestly just didn't feel right to me, but I was so confused I thought maybe I just had to get used to it. The more I engaged in this lifestyle, the more comfortable I became with my new identity. But I still had conflicting feelings—maybe what I was doing wasn't right. I struggled with wondering if my gay tendencies were learned rather than just the way I was born. The confusion of it all was so excruciating I began to increase my drug and alcohol use to suppress the internal battle I was fighting.

Soon my struggles led me to try to seek some spiritual answers. I felt really lost and wanted to know if there was a way to feel at home within myself instead of always feeling out of place and at odds with everyone and everything. I began talking about this kind of stuff with some friends at work, and they invited me to go to church with them. I admit I found it interesting—the whole thing about going to heaven—gaining peace, joy, and happiness. So I started reading the Bible and getting to know these Christians.

One day I prayed and invited Jesus Christ into my heart. I became a Christian and was excited about God and his Word.

Or so I thought.

Unfortunately, I held a false belief—that I could deliberately sin without intending to change my ways or be truly sorry for my sins. I failed to understand the true reason why I needed a Savior, the consequences of my sins, and the need to repent of my sins. "If we deliberately keep on sinning after we have received the knowledge of the truth, no sacrifice for sins is left, but only a fearful expectation of judgment and of raging fire that will consume the enemies of God" (Hebrews 10:26-27).

At this point I'd chosen to believe I was born gay and God couldn't change my homosexual tendencies. So I

started slipping back into my old lifestyle. I chose to hang around a different group at work, most of whom were gay. They were also drug users. Soon partying seemed more fun than going to church.

I slowly fell away from my faith, and I increasingly convinced myself partying gave me a better high than the peace and joy a relationship with God provides. I began turning to alcohol and then drug after drug to fill the emptiness I felt. I did everything I could get my hands on, including acid, cocaine, crack, crank, crystal methamphet-amine, heroin, mushrooms, speed, and of course, Ecstasy. But nothing was able to take away the immense pain I felt within my soul, and my depression and self-hatred grew worse. The men I would begin to invest in emotionally proved they only wanted me for sex. I felt totally used as I suffered heartache after heartache.

Finally, I lost all self-esteem and bought into the idea that I *was* worthless and no good. I was so miserable I tried punishing myself by cutting and stabbing my wrists and arms. I also increased my drug use dramatically, spend-ing literally thousands of dollars a month on drugs. For instance, I would spend almost $1,000 every weekend on just Ecstasy, not including all the other drugs I was using. I'd been somehow holding down a decent-paying job at a state prison, which helped pay for part of my habit, but I also figured out other ways to get the cash I needed to pay for drugs. I took out numerous credit cards and got cash advances on them. I racked up some serious debt—enough to force me to file for bankruptcy.

My habit was so outrageously expensive I also did something I'm not proud of that made it easier to afford and obtain the drugs I "needed." Since I had no trouble getting guys to sleep with me, I thought, *Why not get some money for it to help pay for my addiction?* So I prostituted myself to guys at the clubs. Some even gave me drugs in exchange for sex.

I got so messed up and unable to function I had to quit my job and go into rehab. Once there I began getting disability checks—which I would spend on drugs. I found people who would get them for me, or when I'd get privileges to go out, I'd head straight to my dealer. I took the chance I wouldn't get tested when I got back, until I inevitably did.

I was kicked out of rehab three times, and by the time I entered for the fourth try, my attorney told me if I got kicked out again, I'd do jail time. I stayed in a program and clean for an entire year.

But as soon as I got out of that program, I immediately started drinking and then eventually using every kind of drug again. The continuous negative thoughts in my head coupled with all the drug use were making me see things and hear voices when no one was there. Finally, a voice convinced me just to get my pathetic life over with. Feeling hopeless and overwhelmed because I couldn't break free from my addictions and tendencies, I attempted suicide for the first of 14 times.

Enduring my attempts to take my life, on top of all the stress of having an addict for a son and brother, was tearing my family apart. My sister and I have a very strong connection where we just know when something is wrong with the other one. One night I'd slashed my wrists really badly; stabbed my arm; and taken prescription pills, street drugs, over-the-counter drugs, and alcohol. My sister had a feeling I was in trouble when I didn't answer my phone, so she had someone break into my apartment, where I was found near death.

Luckily, my parents never had to find me after one of my attempted suicides. They'd been through enough as it was. I lied to and manipulated them many times to get money to buy drugs. They'd gone into debt by believing me when I'd swear if they'd pay for rehab, I'd get clean.

They finally swore they'd never help me again. Eventually, my parents split up, and I felt somewhat responsible for their divorce.

I continued to spiral out of control, racking up two drunk driving arrests, having my new Honda Civic EX repossessed, filing for bankruptcy, and being ordered by a court to do another year in a rehab program. But even after all that, I still continued to use drugs. I was addicted and desperate to free myself...somehow.

Three more years passed. I was in and out of rehab and having severe depression and suicidal thoughts. Then when I experienced the pain of losing a friend who committed suicide—and my boyfriend broke up with me right afterward—I seriously lost it.

I began planning how I'd carry out my final suicide attempt, making sure this time I'd succeed. Just as I was about to go through with it, a friend called me and said she knew I was about to do something really stupid. She made me promise I'd go to church and pray.

I began attending the church where my sister occasionally went. Thankfully, I called her to come and take me to church. No one there knew about my homosexuality and what I was going through.

At the church I went into the youth room because it was empty at the time. It was there I finally, literally, cried out to God for help. I begged God to show me he still loved and cared for me. "I need you to show me *right now* that you love me," I pleaded with him. "Your Word says if I cry out to you for help, you *will* help." Then I asked God's forgiveness and said if he helped me, I'd turn away from my sins and follow him forever.

Then what years of rehabilitation couldn't do for me happened in a split second. As I finished my plea, I felt this amazing sense of peace and comfort. The change I felt was stunning—the relief was just incredible. All those urges I constantly battled with had fallen away from me: The urge to drink and use drugs and all the negative thoughts incessantly going around and around in my mind disappeared in an instant. The desperation I lived with day in and day out for years—a feeling I was way too familiar with—was somehow gone.

It was nothing short of a miracle.

From that day I haven't had the urge to drink or use again, and the negative thoughts I constantly tried to rid myself of by every possible means are all gone.

About two months later I finally lost my homosexual urges as well. Whether I was born that way or had chosen to live a gay lifestyle, I'm not sure. What I do know is many times since, my ex has tried to get back together with me, and I've had guys try to ask me out, but I have no interest in or attraction to them. I really don't believe I ever will again.

The difference between this conversion and the first time was this time I had no doubt I'd sinned against God, needed a Savior, and needed to repent of my sins. By listening to and seeking the truth of Jesus Christ, studying the absolute truths of God's Word, and using the tools I learned at a program called Cleansing Streams, I allowed Jesus to set me free from a living hell.

Although Satan still loves to throw a lot of trials my way, instead of turning away as I did when I was a false convert, I grow stronger in my relationship with Jesus Christ. The outright miracle God worked in my life makes me determined to tell my story to the lost and hopeless.

In the past few months my parents have seen enough change in me to decide to help me again. The change in

143

me has been so phenomenal and undeniable they're actually beginning to take a closer look at Jesus and explore Christianity for themselves. They've also resumed supporting me with my education, and I'm on track to finish college by the end of next year.

I've come from the deepest, darkest places—places I sought to make me feel whole, worthy, happy, and fulfilled but only took me into a darker, more miserable life. For years I tried to escape from myself by getting as high as I could possibly get, but I never felt satisfied or at peace. Now I live in a peace that can't be explained.

Believe me when I say God's ways *are* higher: "As the heavens are higher than the earth, so are my ways higher than your ways and my thoughts than your thoughts" (Isaiah 55:9).

Paul Mishoe

MESMERIZED

*"'I will be found by you,' declares the Lord,
'and will bring you back from captivity.'"*

—Jeremiah 29:14

My parents are not Christians: My father is an atheist, and my mother practices a bit from every religion. As a child I had no clue about who Christ is or about what he did for me. I only heard his name when it was associated with profanity. We went to psychics, had our tarot cards and horoscopes read, and always made sure the stars were in the right paths before making huge decisions.

I remember holding séances for my mom to try to ask her stepfather why he did everything he did to her. We'd use a Ouija board to try to speak to spirits. I was taught to read palms and tarot cards and would frequently read for family members.

When I was nine, I moved across the country and quickly found I didn't fit in with the people at my new school. I wanted so badly to be accepted, to have friends, to be loved—especially at home. My father was verbally abusive to me, always putting me down and yelling at me in front of my friends. It seemed nothing I did was good enough for him. When I made any B's, he'd always tell

me how he only made one B in his entire time in high school.

At my first high school competitive gymnastics meet, I was the only freshman who not only placed but did so in all four events. All my father told me was I looked fat in my leotard.

His put-downs only made me more determined to try to be "cool." I began to go to parties where everyone drank because at least I felt accepted. That's when I found my first boyfriend. Although he was a mean drunk, he was good to me most of the time. But he beat me if he lost a basketball game, if he had a fight with his parents, or if he was just having a bad day. I felt as though I deserved this treatment because through it I would have more friends and more love—I craved acceptance.

He raped me about two months after we began going out. After the rape the rules of our relationship changed: If he wanted to date or have sex with other girls, he could. If I wanted to go out with guys, even if as friends, I wasn't allowed. If he found out I did, he'd beat me.

After eight months of this his family made plans to move to Michigan. I told him I didn't want a relationship with him any longer because I couldn't do a long-distance relationship at 14. He became so angry he beat me with a plastic baseball bat. My skull was fractured, my nose was broken, and I had several stitches, but he was out of my life after that night.

After he left, I felt so alone. I began to sleep with any guy I could. I began to drink heavily. I did anything to avoid the thought that no one wanted to love me. The one thing I had any talent for was gymnastics. In my freshman year of high school I got serious and became the only junior varsity gymnast to compete and place in a meet. After winning 10th place in the vaulting event, I went to my parents looking for their praise. Instead my father told me I looked like a whale in my leotard and I needed to lose weight. My mom just laughed, assuming it was a joke, but I knew otherwise.

Reacting to his comment, I began to work out by running with the track team, conditioning during the guys' team practice, and working out close to 30 hours a week. I went on diets, and when that didn't seem to be effective, I began to binge eat. After binging I would then starve myself for days—and before I knew it—weeks.

A year later a guy in my class asked me out. We began to date, and the abuse began again. I felt like I deserved it because if I were just a better gymnast, if I were just better at school, if I were just a better person, I wouldn't be with men like him.

But when he wanted me to quit, I decided my gymnastics career was more important than a boyfriend, and I stood up to him. I was lucky—all I got was a black eye.

After breaking up with him, I really began to feel as though no one, not even my parents, loved me. Finally, sick of feeling alone and depressed, I tried to take my life the Friday before Thanksgiving. I took 90 pills in a span of 10 minutes on an empty stomach. My parents came home to me blacked out with empty pill bottles surrounding me. They piled me into the car and got me to the ER as fast as they could. It took an hour to pump the pills from my stomach.

After that incident I was forced to go into a psychiatric treatment program for a week and then into an outpatient program for about a month. I also began seeing two different therapists on a regular basis.

I finally became stable enough to return to school, although I was still heavily medicated for depression,

anxiety disorders—you name it. I was actually on 11 different prescriptions every day.

Once back in school I decided to get serious about gymnastics again. Before I knew it, there was talk about me making the varsity squad my senior year. It seemed as if life was finally picking up for me. Then one day at practice I blacked out and threw my knee out. I didn't tell my coach it hurt; I just continued to work out.

About a month later my knee popped out of its socket at tae kwon do, and I was rushed to the emergency center. Four days before I began my senior year I had surgery. This injury forced me out of competitions my senior year.

I had a lot of time on my hands once I wasn't competing in a sport, and I was able to focus on trying to become more social. When a friend at school invited me to go to a youth group meeting at her church, I accepted. What really struck me at the meeting was the obvious love the kids there had for each other. I became mesmerized by what they had and knew I wanted that same love in my life.

So I began to research different religions because I felt religion would fill my emptiness. Meanwhile, I was asked to summer camp with the youth group. I was still searching, feeling hopeless, and basically lacking a desire for life at that point. But somehow I found the motivation to earn the money for camp, and I ended up going.

There I finally discovered who Jesus really is, what he did for me, and that no matter what I did, he'd still love me. I finally realized God had always loved and accepted me for exactly who I am. I'd never experienced this kind of unconditional love and acceptance in my life before. The very idea of it was overwhelming. I began to cry, which was unusual for me because I'd get yelled at for crying in front of my father. I didn't want people to see my tears, to see me weak, but when they did, instead of belittling me, they comforted me. Then the youth minister came over and prayed for me, and right then I accepted Christ into my life.

And my life changed.

Before I left for camp, both my therapists had expressed that if I went away to college, they weren't sure I'd be able to handle life without everything familiar around me—and that would push me to attempt suicide again.

When I returned from camp, I'd been out of therapy for three weeks. When my therapists saw me again, they both told me I glowed and seemed remarkably better. I knew the change in me was because I now had Christ in my life, so I proceeded to share the gospel with them, telling them of this love I'd discovered. Looking for a way to explain the change in me, they considered maybe I'd become bipolar because I seemed so happy now—so consistently "up." Eventually, they concluded I wasn't manic, and I was taken off all my medications for emotional disorders.

God had healed me. It wasn't the medications; it wasn't the help of therapists. God and God alone restored me to complete health, and I've been med-free ever since.

About a month and a half after I stopped taking medication, I moved to a college an hour and a half away. There God provided me with an amazing group of people still near and dear to me. There I also discovered who I really am. Although the road has been bumpy, I know I wouldn't be who I am now without Christ as my focus and the center of my life. He took my brokenness and made

me whole again. He not only showed me love but has also used me to love other people.

I've been to Russia with a ministry team and want to return one day. I'm praying about going with a program where I'd serve there for one to two years.

It's so amazing to look back at where I was and see where I am now. The love I've found is just like the love I recognized at that youth group way back when. And unlike spiritualism and the other religions I searched to find love, I'm certain only Christ's love will forever fulfill me and keep me always wonderfully mesmerized.

Brittany Cantrell

MY CONTINUOUS BATTLE

"I will restore them because I have compassion on them. They will be as though I had not rejected them, for I am the Lord their God and I will answer them."

—Zechariah 10:6

So there I was, my little 10-year-old mind thinking, *What just happened? Why did he do that? Was it wrong?* I wouldn't truly know what happened or understand until I was about 15 years old.

I never thought I could be one of "those" kids—but I was. I always thought, *That could never happen to me—never!* It took me several years to realize it had. I was one of those little kids who'd been sexually abused.

I never really thought a small crush on a boy who was five years older than me would lead to something as awful as that, especially at the age of 10. The worst part was he was someone my family and I trusted.

We took him and his sister to church every Sunday with us. We'd pick them up and take them home. I don't even remember how it all started; all I remember is going into the church nursery, just him and me. The nursery had

those really tall cribs you could crawl under—when you'd play hide-and-seek for example—and no one could easily find you.

"Sarah, come here," he said, motioning me to follow him. We hid underneath one of the cribs, and as I was lying on my back, he lay on top of me and started kissing me and touching me, putting his hands where I wasn't sure they belonged. The pain was almost unbearable. I felt as if somebody was sticking me with a thousand needles.

Then he took my hand and began moving it back and forth on his pants. I had no idea what was going on. This went on for quite some time, on numerous occasions, but I never really knew what was going on or understood why I would continue to do that. The very last time it ever happened, my mom opened the nursery door in the church, looking for this boy and me. He immediately stopped, and we came out from under the crib. My mom asked, "What were you two doing?"

"We were just playing hide-and-seek, Mommy," I said.

I didn't know what to call it. I was scared.

Soon after that, he and his sister stopped coming to church with us.

Years later I started having overwhelming fears of being worthless, not meaning anything to anyone, and just feeling completely alone. All my friends were starting to date or had guys who were constantly chasing after them. I felt worthless and as if no one even cared about me. I felt an emptiness that couldn't be filled.

Then one day when I was about 15, a flood of memories came rushing back to me—about being under that crib with the 15-year-old boy. I'd learned enough about physical relationships between men and women to recognize I'd been sexually abused.

But no matter how I tried to justify that I'd been a victim as a 10-year-old, I struggled every day as I placed the blame on myself. I felt only guilt, so instead of asking God to heal me, all I could think was, *How could God forgive someone who would let that happen to herself? How could he forgive me for letting that happen? How can he accept me?*

I couldn't bring myself to tell my parents or any of my friends. I began to draw away from them in fear of being rejected if they knew what'd happened. I felt no one could ever possibly understand me or what I'd gone through.

Eventually, I started having suicidal thoughts and wanted my life to end. I'd been a Christian almost my entire life, and I just knew those feelings were wrong. These ideas emotionally and spiritually drained me. Eventually, the joy I once had in life was gone.

Then one night my church held special prayer meetings. I knew something was wrong with me and the way I was feeling, and I was desperate for some relief. So I got up the courage to receive a prayer for healing. Standing in that prayer line and having the speaker lead a prayer over me sparked something in my heart and mind.

The next thing I knew, I was surrounded by a group of people, probably 15 to 20 of my friends, including my youth pastors. It was the first time God was able to break through my shell, the wall of protection I'd built around my heart. In that moment I felt God truly cared for me and I wasn't alone.

But those feelings of suicide were still in my mind. I just couldn't get rid of them. I came to my wit's end one

HE IS A GOD OF RECOVERY AND RESTORATION

night. I'd had enough. I didn't want to be alone. I didn't want to feel abandoned anymore. I wanted to be loved. I wanted to have my friends back. I wanted to have my parents back. I wanted my life back!

I sat in my room that night four years ago and cried out, "God, if you're truly there, if you truly care about me, if you want me to live—Lord God, just let me know you're here! Let me know I'm not alone!"

Then came the one and only time I've ever audibly heard God's voice. When I heard it, it was as if he were in the room—as if a friend had come in and sat next to me. He said, "Sarah, it'll be okay...I still love you. I'm here for you."

Hearing that gave me the most comforting feeling I've ever had. It was also one of the most amazing moments I've had with God.

That was all I needed.

From that point on I knew I had something to live for. I chose that night to turn my life around and not look at the things that could haunt me from my past. I chose to press forward and have complete faith in God and who he is and what he can do in my life.

And when I did, God took me from a place of complete brokenness and healed my spirit. He took me from a place of complete shame and disrespect for myself to being the kind of woman he created me to be.

I admit sometimes I recall the past and get those feelings of guilt and worthlessness. That's my continuous battle with my mind. To this day I've only been in one dating relationship, and I feel it's because of the abuse I went through. But no matter what happened, I know it wasn't my fault. I just need to remember to give God my troubles and allow him to continue his work in my life. And God is continuing to heal my heart and mind with each passing day. I believe now, more than ever, God can restore us and help us recover from the hurts of our past.

Sarah Packard

STITCHES, SCARS, AND SURVIVAL

> *"The Lord does not look at the things man looks at. Man looks at the outward appearance, but the Lord looks at the heart."*
>
> —1 Samuel 16:7

Of the four kids in my family, I'm the only girl. The closest girl in my extended family is a cousin named Amy who lives in Pocatello, Idaho. When my oldest brother, Trever, decided to visit Amy's dad, Mark, I was packed and ready to go—even though I wasn't invited. This one trip changed my entire perspective on life.

My brother was originally going to take his small compact car on the four-hour drive, but because my two older brothers and I were going along, Mom offered her Chevrolet Astro Van, feeling it would provide a safer, more comfortable ride. It's amazing how God works.

We had a great time with our cousins. The boys all played basketball, and I stayed in the house with the girls and did crafty things. We stayed the night there, with our return planned for the following day. It was really hard for us to leave because of the fun we were having. Finally, at noon we left our cousins' house with Trever in the driver's seat.

While driving out of Pocatello, you encounter an extremely long stretch of road ambling for miles with no visual stimuli; it's known as the "Bermuda Triangle." Trever had driven this road many times before. Even though he'd had a good night's rest prior to our departure, the temptation to doze off was very strong. The rest of us were asleep, and not wanting to wake us, he didn't open a window or turn up the radio or use any other tactic to help him stay awake. Soon Trever became very groggy; he started to nod off. That's when the car swerved off the side of the road. My brother Brandon, who was in the front seat, immediately woke up and yelled, "TREVER, LOOK OUT!"

Trever awoke with a jerk, grabbed the wheel, and overcorrected, which flipped the car into a roll. We rolled and then skidded along the road on the side of the car.

Once the car stopped moving, Trever removed his seat belt and crawled out of the car. Emotionally, he was aching, but physically he only had a small cut on his forehead and a small piece of glass stuck in his hand.

Trent, my brother who'd been in the back seat, had to crawl through a broken window to get out of the car. His left leg and left hand had been scraped along the road after the window shattered; he was bleeding severely. About a quarter of an inch of bone was scraped off his left femur as he crawled through the shattered window. But over the next few months he felt blessed as he went through surgeries, therapy, and healing.

Brandon, my brother who'd been in the front seat, flew out the front window, landed on an uphill slope, and watched everything. He hadn't had his seat belt on, which proved to be a lifesaver—at least this time—because the sliding door sliced through the seat he'd been occupying. When the car landed from its flip in the air, it landed

straight down on the side where Brandon had been sitting. It would've crushed him!

I wish I could say I was as smart as Trever and had worn my seat belt, but I can't. The doctors and our family came to believe I hit my pelvis on the car roof light. Then I flew out the window and landed about 20 yards down the road. My cotton shorts and T-shirt were not assets for my landing. My brother described it: "She scraped along the side of the road, and the right side of her rear end was on her stomach."

The people who'd been driving behind us stopped to give assistance; they had a cell phone with them, which was rare in 1996. Trever called my father and was hysterical as he tried to explain what'd happened. The woman who owned the phone took it from Trever and told my father about the accident from her viewpoint. My parents were panicked, confused, and terrified. All they knew was one child was going be taken to the hospital in an ambulance, another would be airlifted to the hospital for immediate surgery, and the other two had minimal injuries.

Although I don't remember any of the actual accident or the flight, I've heard many stories of my actions and reactions. I wouldn't let the EMTs put me in the helicopter until a prayer was said on my behalf. Trever offered a prayer for me. I consistently asked the pilot if he was sure he'd completed his schooling and told him he could use a few more lessons because the ride was so bumpy.

Once the helicopter arrived at the hospital, I was rushed inside. I remember hearing the helicopter pilot making the comment "This girl deserves to live" as I was rushed into surgery. As I was being pushed on a stretcher down the long hallway, I questioned the lady pushing it. I asked, "My mom and dad haven't arrived yet, but I know my heavenly Father will take good care of me, won't he?"

The lady didn't know how to answer my question. She tearfully told this remark to my mom when my parents arrived at the hospital hours later.

After the surgery I was placed on life support. Within the following 12 hours I received more than 14 units of blood. I was in bandages from head to toe, with my right leg in a splint.

The next morning when I was stable enough to have a second airlift, I was flown to Primary Children's Hospital in Salt Lake City, Utah.

The next 60 days were a nightmare and a miracle at the same time. I went through struggles with yeast in my blood stream, a blood clot, a blocked liver duct, a broken right femur, pancreatitis, more than 100 stitches in my left thigh, numerous other stitches in small places all over my body, intense physical therapy, and no skin on my backside. I was treated as a burn patient and had to have my back, from my shoulders to my thighs, scrubbed and treated twice a day. Every night I would ask my father for a blessing or to pray with me. I often asked my relatives to pray with me. My heart was touched at various moments when I heard about my local church holding fasts for me and my family. But my trials didn't end even after I was released from the hospital in October.

My left knee was a source of excruciating pain. During the accident my kneecap had become detached. When it was healing, it had adhered to the outside of my knee. I was forced into intense physical therapy so I could walk again, but the therapy was wearing down the cradle my kneecap rested in.

In November I was taken into surgery to receive a skin and muscle graft. The doctor cut the muscle in my left calf and flipped it over my kneecap so my kneecap could receive a rich blood supply. In December I had sur-

gery again. Then finally in January my kneecap rejected the graft and was proclaimed dead. It sounds funny that your bones can die, but my leg wouldn't accept the cap back into its original space, so the doctors finally had to remove my kneecap.

I've always had empathy for people with disabilities, especially those with problems affecting their appearance. But now I really know what it feels like to be stared at. I still have problems with people staring at my scars whenever I wear shorts or go swimming.

This experience taught me so much about people helping each other and about myself. I know the meaning of faith, prayer, and determination. I've overcome a lot of problems—which has made me a better person. I know now I can make the best of any situation that comes my way.

During my hardest and darkest moments of college life I've turned to my brother Brandon and had him there to offer me a blessing or pray with me and give me spiritual advice. He and my other two brothers are my closest friends. The best times I've had in my life have been with them at family meals, family vacations, and during family prayer.

I've had boys stop dating me when they've discovered my scars. I've had to pass on certain athletic activities, and I haven't had gym class since I was 11 years old. I may have a bad knee, but it still bends, and bends often, as I offer God thanks for the life I have.

I have scars all over my body, but I'm not too concerned with having physical weakness—I just try to keep what's on the inside beautiful.

Sarah Porter

ALL THE BROKEN PIECES

> *"You never let me tumble over the edge into nothing. But my sins you let go of, threw them over your shoulder—good riddance! The dead don't thank you, and choirs don't sing praises from the morgue. Those buried six feet under don't witness to your faithful ways. It's the living—live men, live women— who thank you, just as I'm doing right now."*
>
> —Isaiah 38:17-19, *The Message*

When I was 13, I had my first experience with God. I went to a rocked-up church where young people hung out every Friday night, and I met the most awesome people who encouraged me in my walk with Jesus. I went to camps; I went to seminars, prayer meetings, worship. You name it—I was there. Everyone at my church knew me. I spent hours in God's Word, prayed consistently: I basically lived and breathed God. People use to say I was on "Holy Spirit steroids"! My walk was strong.

Then something happened.

It was New Year's Eve, and my gran had just passed away. I was 15. That night I went to a party with my cousins and had my first real taste of "life." Peer pressure got

HE IS A GOD OF RECOVERY AND RESTORATION

the better of me, and for the first time ever I let it rule me. I forgot for one night about everything I stood for—and I started drinking.

Soon I found myself alone with a boy who apparently thought I was a "hottie" and hoped he might just get a little bit of action. Maybe it was because I was drunk; maybe it was just his plan the whole night; maybe it was because I said no but couldn't do anything about it. But I remember walking home from that party a completely different person. I'd been raped.

I dealt with it as best I could and didn't tell anyone— just God. I couldn't tell anyone at my church because I couldn't bear how disappointed they'd be in my actions. I couldn't tell my parents because I didn't want to be grounded, and I definitely didn't want to have them press charges because I'd have to see that guy's face again. And I didn't tell my friends because I still wanted them thinking I was as innocent as the rest of them.

So I put on my happy face. I tried really hard to forget about it and focus on repenting. As soon as I thought I'd dealt with everything, I met another boy. It became very evident I hadn't dealt with much at all. We dated for three months, and because of my insecurities and unwillingness to become close in any way, he broke up with me.

My reaction? I stopped eating for four months and became bulimic not long after. I hid food in the backs of closets for weeks on end, until the smell was unbearable, and I'd sneak it out of the house, most of the time wrapped up in paper disguised as "paperwork," and dispose of it.

My life of secrecy continued for months. I was painfully sick and became physically worn out. That's when the depression sank in. *I wouldn't have to deal with the consequences if I were dead, would I?* I asked this every day.

Then I began hurting myself, first in ways that just made me feel a little pain so I could take the focus off my emotions. A scratch here or there turned into an addiction. Every time I became stressed, I had to cut. The wounds became deeper and the scars underneath more and more painful every day.

After about a year of secrecy, cutting, and bad eating habits or not eating at all, it all came crashing to the surface. I was soon in and out of hospitals, sometimes for weeks, sometimes for days. Sometimes I'd go in just to be bandaged up at 3 a.m. and sent home again.

My parents were great through it all—amazingly supportive. I don't know where I'd be without them. But in the midst of all my hurt, I'd forgotten who God was. When I really should've been crying out to God, I didn't want to know him. I stopped praying; in fact, I stopped living.

As one after another of my friends abandoned me, I became more and more lost. I was on four different types of medication for my thoughts and feelings. Suicide had become my desire. I planned and then carried out a series of ways to try to kill myself. When I was allowed to leave the hospital for half days, I'd sneak back supplies of medicine and try to overdose. I'd make deeper cuts on my body in an attempt to bleed to death. I'd hold my breath till I passed out. And then I'd wake up every time and cry to God to just let me die.

But he didn't.

I had few friends left by the third year of my hospitalization, but one who was a Christian visited me in the hospital. When I was at my very lowest, she just sat next to me. I don't think she ever stopped praying for me. She'd often bring me pens and paper and music, and then some days she'd sneak her guitar in to sing me songs,

songs that showed God's love for me, songs that showed how much what I was doing hurt her.

I'd always wanted to experience some divine appointment—a huge God encounter after which I'd be just fine. But it was more than a year after I was out of the hospital before I experienced something remotely like that.

Slowly, I started eating again and stopped cutting, and life seemed a little hopeful...but I still didn't have God—or maybe I didn't want him. I felt so messed up and even more worthless I went from being an obsessive, eating, cutting, suicidal girl into a partygoer and drunk. I turned from cutting to drinking to numb the pain. I turned to sex with anyone who made me feel better. And my suicidal attempts were still there in many ways: I drank hoping I wouldn't wake up, and if I did, well, I'd try again the next weekend. It was a vicious cycle, and my life got no better—just different.

Three and a half years passed, and I was just as messed up as the night my innocence was stolen. Hurt and confused, I knew I desperately needed God.

And then it happened—not quite like I'd expected. No angels, no obvious miracle, no white light shining around me, and no background music. But when I was in the hospital, I'd been told I'd never be able to conceive children. The news totally crushed me. One of my dreams as a little girl was to grow up, get married, and have babies. But during the height of my partying, I became pregnant after a one-night stand. For three months I carried around a baby, and I didn't even know it until I miscarried.

Instead of feeling even more disappointment and self-pity, I saw hope. I felt God had used the situation to show me he was still there. And in the midst of my despair God was able to shine his light through the darkness I'd come to live in and call me back at last. And this time I finally, really listened.

The following Sunday I was in church and on my knees repenting.

It took a long time for my body to recover from what I put it through, but in my heart I knew God was taking care of me. I was no longer at the mercy of my own hands but in the merciful hands of God. He nurtured me and put all the broken pieces back together.

And through the process of restoration I finally recovered from a life of hate, sadness, anger, and a bleak future. I've gained a life filled with joy, hope, and a bright future.

God is so good.

Louise Russell

PIECE BY PIECE

"The Lord himself goes before you and will be with you; he will never leave you nor forsake you. Do not be afraid; do not be discouraged."

—Deuteronomy 31:8

A friend of mine once said, "I'll have to come over and use your scissors sometime. It'd be totally fun."

Fun was the last thing on my mind as I continued to cut deep gashes into my arms. I hated what I was doing and hated my life. I felt as if I were in a crowded room, screaming at the top of my lungs with no one even bothering to look. I wanted to die. I wanted to cut away the pain I was feeling inside and just end my life right then and there.

The pain had two sources. My dad was an alcoholic, and he seemed not to care about me or my family. My boyfriend was very controlling, and I felt I had no way out of the relationship. He told me if I broke up with him, he'd commit suicide. I was so scared he actually might, I stayed with him for as long as I could stand it.

TRUE VOL.2

I didn't love my boyfriend; I was obsessed with him. I was always depressed and miserable when I was with him. He had a way of always making me feel bad about myself, which led to my cutting.

One night I just couldn't stand his making me feel down, so I thought the only way out was to give up on life altogether. I stood with pills in hand, taking one after another. Soon I got really tired and went to lie down for a while. The whole night I was really scared my life was actually going to end. I woke up the next morning thanking God for saving me from this mistake. I thought maybe from this experience God would help me, and I wouldn't be so miserable all the time. Boy, was I wrong! The pills stopped but the cutting didn't.

I went to church every Sunday but hadn't asked why God was making me feel as if the only way to find relief was to leave this world completely. Cutting became my addiction, my only way out of the life I had no control over. It made me feel happy and secure. Sometimes I actually enjoyed watching blood drip down my arm.

My parents soon found out I was doing this to myself as did half the kids at school. My mom put me in therapy, and I felt as if everyone were talking about me behind my back. I was ashamed and embarrassed, and most important, I knew how upset God must've been with me. On top of that, therapy didn't help; it only made me worse. I hated going, and I hated how after all the shame and disappointment I continued to cut myself.

Then I found out I wasn't the only one doing this. My boyfriend was as well. Even though we were both really unhappy, we stayed together. I broke up with him a number of times, but he always somehow talked me into going back out with him every time.

I became so miserable I started to burn my arms as well. No matter how hard I tried and no matter how hard people tried to talk me out of it, I couldn't stop. Finally, I broke down and told my mom everything that had been going on in my life. She started crying, demanding I show her my arm. I was crying just as hard as I showed her. She yelled for my dad to come into my room and made me show him, too. All he did was yell and scream at me, asking me why I was doing this to myself. I didn't have an answer for him.

I cried myself to sleep that night, thinking about how much pain I was causing everyone, myself included. I lay awake all night just praying to God. I asked him why he'd placed this burden on me and prayed he would just take all my pain and fears away. I actually begged God to help me stop hurting myself.

The next week I somehow found the strength to break up with my boyfriend. I decided no matter what he said to me, I was never going to get back together with him. For months after, it seemed as if his goal was to make my life a living hell, but I struggled and got through it. No matter what he or any of his friends said to me, I knew I couldn't go back to cutting myself. So whenever I felt depressed, I went straight to my prayer book and prayed. And in a matter of minutes I'd feel 100 percent better.

My dad finally stopped drinking, and in a grand total of two years my life was finally being put back together piece by piece.

People sometimes ask, "If God loves us so much, why does he cause such horrible things to happen in our lives?" I believe it's not God's doing. He gives us free choice. And if hard times didn't happen in our lives, we'd never need God.

As time goes on, I wonder where I'd be now if God hadn't been there for me. If I've learned anything from my experiences, I now know I'll never give up on God because God will never give up on me.

Katie Skarvinko

HE IS A GOD OF CONSTANT COMPANIONSHIP.

"O Lord, you have examined my heart and know everything about me. You know when I sit down or stand up. You know my every thought when far away. You chart the path ahead of me and tell me where to stop and rest. Every moment you know where I am. You know what I am going to say even before I say it, Lord. You both precede and follow me. You place your hand of blessing on my head...How precious are your thoughts about me, O God! They are innumerable! I can't even count them; they outnumber the grains of sand! And when I wake up in the morning, you are still with me!"
—Psalm 139:1-5, 17-18, NLT

THE VOICE INSIDE

"'I will never leave you nor forsake you.'"

—Hebrews 13:5, ESV

I stared blankly at the computer screen. Tears welled up in my eyes, spilling over onto my cheeks. The darkness of the room slowly crept inside my heart as it sank. The chilling silence seemed deafening as the cursor blinked, waiting for a response. He was breaking up with me.

He'd pursued and won my heart over a matter of months, introducing me to new and exciting levels of commitment and genuine acceptance. We became fast friends, growing in conversation and love for one another. Though we had our share of heartaches, fears, and disappointments, we remained close and persevered through it all.

Yet something inside me began to shift, and my heart began to feel restless. The deeper our relationship grew, the more problems began to surface. I soon realized we differed in our spiritual lives, and I was actually being pulled away from my once-strong convictions. He started fighting me on spiritual issues, and his lack of desire for a relationship with God became evident. I found myself caught between my desire for God and my desire for the

man I was dating. Did I have to choose? Why couldn't I just enjoy a relationship with both? Yet I knew deep within my spirit I could never continue dating him while being fully committed to God; I was being dragged down with each passing day.

However, I chose to ignore the decision because it was too difficult to think about. I smothered my dilemma and continued with my relationship, which only went from bad to worse over the course of two years.

The glow from the computer screen was obnoxious and seemed to laugh at my feeble attempt to hold on tight to everything dear. This was my chance to get out of a bad relationship. So why was it so hard?

Slowly, my stiff and trembling fingers punched out a response on the keyboard. "Okay," I muttered to myself as I agreed to end the relationship. It was over. And just like that he was gone from my life. He left me to deal with the broken pieces. Frustrated, I flipped the switch and shut off my monitor.

I sat in the dark, trying to silence the sound of my crying. The only other sound was the gentle breathing of my roommate, sleeping peacefully behind me. Outside the wind blew softly as if to reassure me I'd done the right thing. Everything seemed so still and quiet, trying to comfort me. Yet inside I was boiling.

It's not fair! I wanted to shout. As if a wave were crashing down around me, I began to drown in my sorrow. Who was I supposed to run to when trouble came? Who was I supposed to turn to when I needed help? No longer would someone be there for me the way a boyfriend is. My frustration soon turned to anger. I marched to my bed and collapsed into it, thrusting the covers under my chin. I angrily glared at the ceiling in defiance, as if it were God's fault this'd happened.

Why did we have to break up? I've lost everyone dear to me! I screamed inside. Not only had I just lost my boyfriend, but my dad had also recently died from a sudden heart attack. My boyfriend had been the one who comforted me and helped me through my grief. He'd been my safety, my security. Tears of grief, loneliness, and hopelessness flowed onto my small pillow. *Why couldn't you have let me keep him? I* cried to God. *I've been through so many hard times, and he's been with me through them all!*

And then I heard it. Powerful and intense yet just as kind and gentle, a voice interrupted my thoughts: "So have I."

I froze. A real voice. A voice I didn't know and had no control over. It was not an audible voice, yet it was just as real as my own. And as soon as the voice spoke, I knew who it was. Scared, frightened, confused as to what was going on and still upset, I answered.

Well, no offense, God, I thought, *but why can't I just rely on a physical person? Why does it always have to be spiritual?* I grimaced as soon as the thoughts left me, hoping I hadn't offended God. I really wanted to rely on him, but it's hard to depend on someone I can't see.

Immediately, I heard it again. His voice, distinct and separate from my own, spoke directly to me.

"Because physical people fade," God answered. "They can be gone in an instant and can't always be there for you. But I can. I will never leave you nor forsake you."

God's words settled across my heart, impacting me with force. I lay silent and still before God, waiting to see if he'd say anything more, but he never did.

Though our conversation had been short, I was in awe. My spirit calmed, softly at first and then more and more powerfully. A peace settled over me and quieted my anxious mind. I remained still for what seemed like hours, afraid to move and disrupt the surreal moment.

Finally, I fumbled for a pen in the dark, quickly writing down word for word what I'd heard so I'd never forget God's answers. Only later I discovered he'd answered me from Hebrews 13:5, a verse I'd never read before. How could I have received answers from Scriptures I'd never read, from a verse I never knew existed? But I had.

God had answered my questions with his own voice. And with his words I received the guidance I'd so desperately needed. Though I'd lost someone close to me, I had someone even closer whom I could depend on—someone who was even more personal than I'd realized. Someone who had, for a moment, whispered to me in the darkness and given me a promise. God would never leave me nor forsake me.

Rachel Giffin

SINKING SAND

"Do not put your trust in princes, in mortal men, who cannot save. When their spirit departs, they return to the ground; on that very day their plans come to nothing. Blessed is he whose help is the God of Jacob, whose hope is in the Lord his God, the Maker of heaven and earth, the sea, and everything in them—the Lord, who remains faithful forever."

—Psalm 146:3-6

I paced the floor and glared at the black-rimmed clock in the school cafeteria. I was waiting for my boyfriend Jason. He was supposed to meet me for lunch, but he was late, as usual.

I went looking for him, and as I walked around the corner, near the science lab, I saw him. He was walking hand in hand with my best friend Jill!

She had the decency to look away in shame, but he looked me in the eye, smiled a cruel smile, and casually said, "Hi, Nance." They just kept walking. I fell against the wall as my knees and heart folded.

At first I was numb to the pain, but soon the anger of the double betrayal began to simmer and then boil.

I went through the rest of my classes with a steeled determination not to cry. I made it all the way home. As I locked the door to my bedroom, I cried until I was empty of tears.

Jason had been my whole world. He was one of the most popular guys at school, and when I was with him, I felt important. I liked being defined as "Jason's girlfriend," partly because I hadn't developed any other definition of myself.

I thought, *How could he betray me so easily? And with Jill!* She'd been a close friend since seventh grade, and I didn't understand how she could've done this to me.

I thought my life was over. I felt like less than nothing.

I tried to pray, but I couldn't get my mouth to form any words. I picked up the Bible by my nightstand and held it to my chest as I simply said, "Help me, God." Then I felt better. Stronger. I opened to Hebrews 13:5: "For he himself has said, 'I will never leave you or forsake you'" (CSB). Then I thought of a song we often sang at church: "On Christ the solid rock I stand; all other ground is sinking sand." I'd been standing on Jason—and he'd crumbled.

In the next few months I started to rebuild my life and develop my own identity. I auditioned for a part in a play and was thrilled to get Townswoman #3. I didn't have any lines, but I was happy just to be part of the team and make new friends. Jill was the lead character in the play, and at first it was hard to be around her, but as time went on, we became friends again.

I started to discover things about myself—hidden treasures. I took a creative writing class and poured myself into it. I was the only one in the class who got an A+. I also volunteered to teach a children's Bible study, got involved in my church's youth group, and took a part-time job at a restaurant.

That winter I learned a valuable lesson as I watched Jason betray Jill and move on to his next victim.

I never again measured my worth by another person's loyalty to me. As I learned to stand on God's love and use the gifts he's given me, I saw that God is a consistent and unfailing friend. I also learned people will disappoint me, and I'll disappoint myself, but God will never leave me or betray me.

I was recently in contact with Jason through a class reunion, and I learned he's struggling to hold his third marriage together. I married a wonderful man I met while I was attending Bible college, and we recently celebrated our 25th wedding anniversary. I can honestly say I'm thankful my world crumbled while I was in high school because I rebuilt it on Christ, the solid rock.

Nancy C. Anderson

CLOSER TO THE FIRE

> *"Ask and it will be given to you; seek and you will find; knock and the door will be opened to you."*
>
> —Matthew 7:7

My parents told me I was a Christian, so that's what I always called myself. I believed in Jesus and that he died, came back, and all that stuff, but I kept my faith bottled up for Sundays at church and Wednesdays at Bible study. I wasn't *really* a Christian; I was a hypocrite who was, in reality, running *away* from God.

I would lie, cheat, spread rumors, and make fun of people I hardly knew. Not only did I trash my enemies behind their backs, but I also often deliberately hurt my friends—by doing so I eliminated what little faith I had.

A couple of times I tried getting reconnected with God. I'd get really inspired by something and would come home, pray, and promise to become a better person. Within a couple of days, though, I'd be back to my bad habits. Then I'd blame God for my drifting away. I figured if God cared about me at all, he'd help me stay committed to him. His love became a fairy tale I went along with on Sunday mornings.

Summer meant that time for Camp Calvin Crest (or "God Camp" as I less lovingly referred to it) would come around, and my friends from church always went. I'd gone one summer and come home on a spiritual high, but I'd drifted away from that. Plus, in my mind, God had betrayed me. He hadn't come running to me when I called him, so why should I go running to him? I'd be going to a camp full of people who knew Jesus, and they wouldn't understand if I said I didn't.

So I decided I wasn't going to go under any circumstances. But it gets really obnoxious when you have your church friends interrogating you, asking, "Why aren't you coming?!" I didn't want to tell anybody, including my parents, who were also pressuring me, about the struggles I'd been having with my faith.

So I gave in.

When I got to camp, I immediately bonded with the other girls in my cabin. I quickly learned that my preconceptions about having a cabin full of "church girls" were wrong. Some of these girls were just as confused as I was, some of them even more. *Maybe this won't be so bad*, I found myself thinking. And the funny thing is, I eventually found out it wasn't.

One night at campfire one of our counselors gave her testimony. Throughout the entire 15 minutes, she kept on telling us, "God loves you. God loves you. No matter what, God loves you." I didn't get it. Of all the people in the world who truly acted like Christians, why would God choose to love me? I didn't live for God—why would he want to bother with me? But the way this girl said it, I *had* to believe her: She was so convincing it was impossible not to. Something inside me broke open, and a crack of light began to creep into my heart. The light created warmth so soothing and comforting I wanted more of it. I decided I'd begin to open up to God and see what happened.

I did a lot of soul-searching the next day, and by the time campfire rolled around the next evening, I felt ready at last to ask God to enter my heart. I was so excited, yet I still didn't really think it would happen. It was like wanting to win the lottery. You hope for it, even pray for it, but you doubt it'll ever happen to you.

I was wrong.

That night Chad and Jenna, codirectors of the camp, did a skit about emotional baggage and how Jesus asks us to give it to him and let him carry it. He's stronger than we are, and he can handle it. They also told us that for God to forgive us, we needed to first forgive ourselves.

And that's when it hit me. I realized I'd painted myself into a corner by lashing out at others and then not being able to forgive myself for it. I recognized I didn't want others to see my weaknesses, so I kept hurting people because I was hurt. I was now seeing that God could help me break the cycle, and I could allow him to be my friend. I realized I'd been longing for his love all along, even when I tried pushing him and all my friends away. Was I just afraid of being loved, or did I think I didn't deserve it?

Suddenly, none of those things held me back anymore. Not the people I'd hurt, the battles with my friends, or the emotional scars I wore from those battles—because God's power and love were so much bigger than all of that. The feeling was so overwhelming I started to cry, just a little at first. But then Chad started talking about commitment and running to the cross, which represented ultimate faith, and he described seeing Jesus standing there with open arms. I don't really remember half of the other things he said, but I just remember sobbing so much I probably could've drowned the whole camp if my friends hadn't let me use their shirts as tissues. When he was done talking, he asked if anyone would like to make a commitment.

No one spoke. After a while one of the guys got up and just moved closer to the fire. I grabbed the two girls on either side of me and dragged them up to sit by him, and we all sat staring into the flames. Others quickly followed us. It was as if somehow God was in the fire, and we all just wanted to be closer to him, to feel the warmth of his presence fill the empty, cold places inside.

While I was looking around the fire at the people who had, in the past couple of days, become some of my best friends, I could really see the face of Jesus. It was like a pinball machine. Jesus was the ball, and whenever he hit a bumper—a person's heart— she'd light up. Some faces were streaked with tears; others were just staring into the flames, not blinking despite the smoke.

Soon almost all of us had moved up closer to the fire. Then I got this thought that must've come from God. *If you don't talk now, you'll regret it. If you don't commit now, you never will.* So after working on getting some guts, I said, "Tonight I want to commit to running. I want to run to the cross, and I don't ever want to turn back."

The rest of the week went by too fast. I was scared to go home because I didn't want to lose what I'd gained over those six days.

My first test came right away.

The day after I got home, one of my school friends wanted me to come over. We were bored, so she decided to show me this clip on the Web of a guy saying, "This is gay. That's gay. Everything is ----ing gay!" It drove me crazy. I just sat there with my arms crossed while she laughed her head off.

"What's wrong with you?" she asked.

"I'm still at church camp," I replied, longing to be where I'd at first refused to go. Who would've thought?

"Well, when are you coming back?" she asked with impatience.

When I got home, I realized I wasn't coming back. I'd dumped all the negative stuff in me on Jesus. I'd left the person she'd been friends with in those flames.

That night I sent her an e-mail telling her all of this. Going back was turning my back on God, and I wasn't willing to do that again.

In no time at all my "friend" abandoned me and actually said she couldn't stand me anymore. But Jesus still loves me. His friendship will last forever.

That's really all that matters.

Madeline Shomos

SUFFICIENT FOR ME

> *"My grace is sufficient for you, for my power is made perfect in weakness."*
>
> —2 Corinthians 12:9

My friends are always telling me how fun it is to make out with guys.

Well, I wouldn't know.

I'm almost 20 years old, and I've never kissed anyone. Not only that, but I've never been in a real relationship with anyone of the opposite sex. It's not because I'm not attractive, or funny, or nice—it's...well, actually, I really don't know why. I'm definitely not one of those girls who has to have a boyfriend to complete her or anything, but every once in a while it'd be nice to know someone likes me, thinks I'm cute or pretty, or just wants to be around me.

I was talking to one of my friends the other day, and she said, attempting to comfort me, "Well, it's okay that you're single; Jesus can be your boyfriend."

What's that supposed to mean? I want to remind people who say this that I've never even been on a date

and ask them if it'd look a little funny to see me with my arm around no one at the movies or dancing with myself at a school dance. Of course it would because God can't really be my boyfriend, and I'm not sure I really like that image anyway. To be honest, it's sort of weird.

A new fad is going around—I guess it's really not that new to some people, but for me it is. Now that my friends and I have left high school and moved on to the bigger and better place we call college, our conversations have moved from talking about who we think is cute to who we made out with last night. I go to a small Christian college in Illinois, but my friends from high school are all at huge state schools like the University of Illinois or Michigan State or Iowa, so they're into that sort of thing. You know—the parties, drinking, boys, and making out.

You can see how this puts me in an odd spot, as I've never kissed anyone. I can't really participate in their conversations. But being drunk and making out with random guys doesn't sound that fun to me.

Sometimes my friends don't even know these guys' names, let alone ever talk to them again. I try really hard not to be annoying by bringing up the whole "God thing"; I try to lead by example instead, but I don't think my friends view my life philosophy as all that fun.

So where does that leave me? Stuck in the middle, that's where. "Everyone is doing it." That's a popular slogan, but what does it mean? I should give part of myself away to random guys I'll never talk to again? I should "live it up" while I can? God doesn't call Christians to that type of life; he wants something better for us. Honestly, I want something better for myself. Then when I get married, I can know I saved myself completely for my husband.

Pure. Naive. Single. Yes, I'm all of that, but I've been learning through this process of being single that God is sufficient for me. He really is all I need and everything I could ever want.

Sometimes I do sort of wish I could just kiss someone, *anyone*. I think it might be nice to have a boyfriend, someone who loves me like that. But God has been sufficient for me, and God will be sufficient for me. Obviously, I can't kiss or hug God, but I can talk to him, cry to him, and walk with him, and he NEVER leaves.

Don't worry—this story doesn't end with me coming to grips with my singleness, moving to Rome, and magically finding a boyfriend who looks just like a movie star—that's not real life. I'm still single, and I'm pretty sure I will be for at least a while yet, but I've realized some truths about God that continually strike me and give me peace.

I know God has someone special picked out for me, so all my worrying about "finding the right guy" is stupid. God knows who my future husband is, and feeling bad about being single won't bring him here any faster. Most important, God *does* have a plan for me. I can't see it right now, but I know it's going to be really awesome.

Amanda Reese

LIVING FORTRESS

> *"Love comes from God, and when we love each other, it shows that we have been given new life. We are now God's children, and we know him. God is love, and anyone who doesn't love others has never known him."*
>
> —1 John 4:7-8, CEV

I always knew someone existed in the universe, perhaps called God or Jesus, but he, she, or it wasn't real to me.

As a child I spent a few Sundays "learning" about this God. But all the puppets and stale crackers and juice I endured while a droning pastor spouted off words written thousands of years ago weren't going to penetrate the walls built around my young heart. The lame music didn't help much, either.

By the time I was 14, I'd become a living fortress, unwilling to allow anyone, especially God, into my life. And I was especially unwilling to let go of my past. I held onto my heartache so tightly it became a wall of bitterness and anger ready to destroy my life and my relationships.

I remembered being a kid with rage and a sense of helplessness as I watched the adults in my life destroy

themselves or each other. These thoughts and hurts began to stack up in my heart.

So when it came to God, I had questions and doubts. Big doubts.

How could there be a God who would let a father abandon his unborn son? How could he allow an innocent child to see such destruction in his family? How could he allow me to witness violence so crushing the images of each specific event make up an album of photos in my mind?

I can still remember watching the man I called Dad hauled off to explain to the police why he threw my mother into the dining room table, breaking her ribs. I'll never forget how she cried as the female officer helped her with her wound while I held onto her. And then there was the time my mom held me up in front of her like a shield because somehow she knew my dad wouldn't dare hit a five-year-old; I remember the look in his eyes as he dropped the shelf on my bedroom floor.

As a preteen I refused to sit by as a new man took the same swings at her, but I wasn't strong enough to protect her, and I only complicated the situation. Now the police were showing up at home one night and at my school the next day to ask me what'd happened.

To protect myself I tried burying my emotions under activity. I focused on schoolwork and art to avoid the memories. I know this sounds strange, but work can be an addiction just like drugs or alcohol. It may be far less destructive, yet it's still just a distraction from what's really happening.

I soon found there were never enough awards or proud words to eliminate the burden I was carrying inside. Even though my family members and teachers often told me what a good person I was and how they were so proud

of me, they simply couldn't see the pain and frustration I was holding deep inside. I couldn't escape my past and had no place to hide. My bedroom with the door shut was my sanctuary.

One morning my mom was brave enough to enter the sanctuary of my room, wake me up, and ask me to go to church with her. It'd been a long time since I'd been there. Memories of bad music and stale crackers came flooding back into my groggy mind. But I didn't scream at her to get out and leave me alone. For some reason I rolled over and said "five more—well, more like 30 more—minutes, Mom."

As I dragged myself out of bed and began getting dressed, the walls around my heart thickened, and my mood turned bitter. Although I was resistant to the whole idea, I decided to go.

As soon as I got to church, I noticed something different about that ordinary day. I could feel my emotions building up throughout the time of worship and the sermon. It was as if the walls around my heart couldn't be any higher, and I had no more room for pain or rejection. Suddenly, I couldn't hold back my tears, no matter how hard I tried.

Although I can't remember the exact words spoken that day, what I do remember was an offer. I had a choice to continue to live with what was beginning to destroy me or acknowledge God and let him destroy my fortress of sorrow. Given the weird change in my emotions and all I'd heard that morning, I believed God actually could do it.

So I pulled just enough of the wall away to let God in. Before I knew what was going on, I began to recall the most painful moments in my past. This trip back in time didn't seem designed to hurt me but more to remind me

God had always been with me, holding and comforting me.

He was just waiting for me to recognize him.

When I gave God a chance to explain about all those awful years, he helped me see things very differently. It was as if a bright light of recognition blazed away in my mind, showing me all the times and ways God was there—for every good and bad experience—no matter how much I tried to deny it.

Instead of thinking God had abandoned me, I suddenly saw how God had worked through people to show me his love, mercy, and kindness. Every time in my life I heard the words *I love you*, God was behind them.

When my mom hugged me, God was behind it.

Whenever someone was proud of what I'd accomplished, God was smiling at his creation.

Every time I felt rejected, God accepted me because I'm his unique creation.

Whenever I chose not to explode with anger at a situation, God had given me patience.

God even worked through a few men he'd strategically placed in my life to teach me. Men like my uncle who was always there to listen, was present at my birth, and to this day calls me just to talk for a while and make sure I'm doing okay.

God showed me the good things the abusive men he'd allowed in my life had taught me. And though they'd caused many of the hurts I was holding, God still loved them, and I could, too.

Sitting in that church pew, I slowly began reasoning that it didn't matter that I didn't know my biological father because I'd always had a heavenly Father guiding my paths. That one final realization helped me choose to follow Jesus.

Right then I accepted God's love, and he accepted my pain.

Once I'd made the decision to follow Christ, I began a journey of healing. As a teenager and young adult, God blessed me with three different male youth leaders and a pastor, each of whom mentored me and taught me how to be a man of God, sometimes through their successes and sometimes through their failures. Participating in church and youth group brought me in contact with several young men who influenced me as we all grew into adults together. I also know God was instrumental in placing the exact women I'd need in my life to help me carry the burden of feeling abandoned and wounded. Still, none of these mentors could replace the love and acceptance I felt when I gave my life to Christ.

That decision has carried me through some awesome highs but also some extreme lows. God has allowed me to realize loved ones will sometimes hurt the people closest to them. And sometimes I'll hurt the people I love most. This has helped me build healthy relationships with those who've caused heartache in my life. Every day I learn how to forgive a little bit more.

The memories of what I've been through and what I've done are still with me. My eyes still well up with tears as I write. However, the memories of my past will never be bigger than Jesus, and the pain will never be bigger than God's love.

My heart soars when I think about the peace God has given me; it soars from the measure of mercy he offers when I'm the one inflicting the pain. It soars because now I know I'm here to be a living fortress for God, not a stronghold for sorrow.

And my heart soars with the hope that I'll use my life to help others find their way home and that they'll choose to let their hearts soar by releasing the pain they were never meant to carry.

Brandon Tamblin

SWIMMING THE WALK

> *"You're familiar with the old written law, 'Love your friend,' and its unwritten companion, 'Hate your enemy.' I'm challenging that. I'm telling you to love your enemies. Let them bring out the best in you, not the worst. When someone gives you a hard time, respond with the energies of prayer, for then you are working out of your true selves, your God-created selves."*

> —Matthew 5:43-45, *The Message*

"Come on, man. Stop being such a friggin' loser!"

They all said it—the eight of them who were there, anyway. Honestly, I couldn't believe I was in that position in the first place. I mean, I was with friends. Sure, it's not as if I'd met them at church or anything, but they all knew my position on things like that.

"Dude, are you gay or something? Ha, ha, ha! He's gay! What a flamer!"

"Hey, guys, come on. You know I just broke up with my girlfriend and—"

"Yeah, because you're gay."

"Just because I don't wanna look at your porn doesn't mean I'm gay."

I couldn't believe my ears. These were the same guys I swam laps with every day. The same ones I was about to swim a relay with, but no matter...I was there and stuck. I was so stuck it was as if my own brothers were betraying me—the same brothers who'd helped me through getting dumped by telling me it wasn't the end of the world and then giving me extra-hard sets to swim out the aggression.

I looked at my watch; we were supposed to be getting pumped up for the swim meet. We were to face our biggest rivals in less than an hour; how could my teammates betray my trust like this at such a crucial time?

I wasn't proud to be a Christian right then. I'd grown up in church my whole life—I'd heard all the stories: "Jesus just gave me strength. It's like he came into the room and spoke for me." Or the angel stories—you might know similar ones: "I was sitting there, praying to God my friends would leave me alone, and all of a sudden all my worries were handled! I didn't know what was going on, but apparently, as my friends told me later, these two big muscular guys were sitting right beside me."

No, none of that happened to me—if only it had. Instead I sat and waited for meet time.

I said, "Hey, guys, I'm sorry. This is who I am; this is what I'm all about. I'm not going to look at the naked women on your computer."

I would like to be able to say they simply listened to what I said, thought rationally, and said, "Wow, yeah, he's right. He's actually standing for what he believes in,

and that's cool." But they kept at it. I sat and watched TV by myself and turned it up to drown out the noise coming from the next room. After wasting their entire pump-up time, they decided to pump up by making fun of me on the walk to the pool.

However, the next part was the true test of my Christianity. The guys started with locker-room talk—which meant tearing me down in front of the other team. I was humiliated. The rest of the night girls looked at me and giggled. Guys made bad jokes and offered me a hand of friendship, pretending that made it all right to set up another joke.

The truth is, I made it through. Guys occasionally referred to it the next week at practice, but after that the comments died a natural death. That's when the cool stuff started to happen. Everybody had known me to be a Christian before that night, but the sad part is some of them had known themselves to be Christians, too. I provided a different perspective on life to a couple of them.

A month after that night, Brent, one of the guys who'd made fun of me, asked me to talk with him after practice. I didn't really have anything to do, so I said I'd give him a ride home. I figured he wanted to tell me about a girl he was interested in, maybe even one of my friends I could hook him up with. I was really surprised when he got in my car and started in about how he had no clue what was going to happen to him because his parents had told him the night before they were planning on getting a divorce. I couldn't believe he was telling me this. Brent and I were teammates and all, but we weren't best friends or anything. He told me he didn't know anywhere else to go.

He said, "I know you pray and all, so I thought maybe you could put in a prayer for me. Maybe you could even pray my parents will stay together at least until I'm out of there."

Now I'd had my one stand earlier in the season, but I wasn't one of those Bible-banging nuts who preached at his friends and converted 10 people a week to Christianity. So I surprised myself when I said, "No problem, Brent. I'll keep you in my prayers. Actually, do you wanna pray right now?" Even more surprising was how quickly and enthusiastically he agreed to it. I prayed, he got out of the car, and I drove home amazed at what'd just happened.

Two weeks later another one of my teammates, Clinton, pulled me aside just before practice. He said, "Hey, I hear you pray for people. Is that right?"

I said, "Yeah, why?"—not sure at this point if I should be lacing up my boxing gloves or pulling out my prayer mat.

He said, "Well, it's really stupid, but ever since Katie and I broke up, I've been scaring myself with the thoughts going through my head. I'll be home alone doing homework or watching TV, and I'll just get the urge to go find my dad's gun and stick it in my mouth and pull the trigger. I dunno. Life just stinks—so anyway, can you pray for me?"

I looked at Clinton and said, "Not only will I pray for you right now, but I'll also keep praying for you. I know how hard it is to lose a girlfriend—times when you're by yourself are the worst. Anytime you need to talk, you've got my number."

I'd turned into the default swim team chaplain without even asking. The funniest part was most of the guys didn't even know the other guys were coming to me, too. But the best part was seeing how God used my standing up for my beliefs to draw others closer to himself. The guys

rejected me at first, but I stayed steady and remained a friend to them, just as God always has for me.

Samuel R. Stephens

AMAGING LOVE

"Greater love has no one than this, that he lay down his life for his friends."

—John 15:13

We were probably 10, though it's hard to believe, and I can still feel the dampness and dirtiness of the attic. My friend Katie found her parents' box of magazines, and we peeked around her to see. As young girls we found the photos funny and strangely curious. I can't remember details, but I do recall knowing that something, somehow, somewhere deep inside of me awakened. Thus, a long, sad journey began.

Around that time I was hanging out with Paula. She lived near a guy whose parents happened to be away during the day. I can still see that round wooden table, all four chairs, two boys, and two girls, including me. I can still feel my heart beating quickly while someone spun the phone. Robby and I were the "lucky" winners. The prize... well, it awaited me under the stairs of his basement.

Riding home afterward with my mom gave me some time to think. My reflections were profound...*Gross! Yuck! Is that what everybody makes such a fuss over?* And yet I was happy I'd had my first real kiss. I didn't talk to

my parents or older siblings—or to anyone else for that matter—about serious things, and therefore, I kept it all inside, wondering about it all.

When I was 12 years old, a friend down the street invited me to church. The youth group was a great place to hang out, and I felt better about myself when we sang and read the Bible. I'll never forget that church bus...or one weird trip. Chris, a good friend, sat next to me and bluntly informed me Bill wanted to go out with me. Suddenly, Bill sat next to me and started rubbing my back. I asked myself, *Did I miss something? What's happening?* Bill never asked me, so I never answered. But I did like Bill, and who wouldn't? He was, after all, the leader in the youth group—outgoing, funny, popular, and very aggressive.

I was the opposite.

Sadly, I can't remember how our relationship became so physical. There's no first time in my memories, rather a blur of unpleasant thoughts and feelings about sex something like this: *Why doesn't this feel right or fun? It's not really what I want, but I love him.*

Bill started getting into the popular crowd during high school. The person who paid the most attention to me, even if it was sexual, was slowly drifting away. I began to hate myself for loving him. I couldn't break free from him, and even though I wanted to walk away, I'd try and then end up just running right back to him.

He gradually just stopped coming around; I never received a good-bye or explanation. Then began a heartache so deep and insecurity so strong no amount of drinking or sex could ease them.

A lot happened between those years and furthered the blow. I accidentally started a fire that almost burned down our house. Luckily, my brother woke up during the fire and got out unharmed, escaping death by just a few minutes.

My old friend Paula tried to kill herself and regretted it...too late. Bill's dad killed himself, too.

Once more I was alone with no answers.

There I was, about to graduate from high school and move on to what can be a very exciting time in life, but sadly, I hated myself and my life.

I went off to college and tried to make the best of it. I decided I'd be more social and see if I could make some new friends. Finally, my efforts paid off, and I started hanging out with the "popular people." I was also getting straight As by studying hard during the week, even though I was partying harder on weekends. When I stopped and looked at my routine, I realized I was going nowhere fast.

Deep down was a longing I couldn't ignore. I began having all kinds of questions relating to my existence and the purpose of life. *Why am I here? How did I get here? What's going to happen when I die?* Then something, somehow, somewhere deep inside of me awakened. I felt driven to dig out my Bible and search for answers, thinking if answers were in there, I'd recognize them. I couldn't shake the longing I had to know the God who created me. And so I prayed, asking God to show me if he was real. And I threw in the request not to let me die without knowing him.

It's crazy how my life suddenly became more vibrant and in tune with everything. It seemed as if various things throughout my days pointed to the existence of a Creator: a song, a bird, a book.

That summer I worked as a lifeguard. One particular day people on both sides of the lifeguard stand were playing music. On one side a Christian family was playing their music about...well, you know. On the other side of me was music I liked. Somehow those tunes just deepened my despair. Everything seemed so down about those songs: "Love bites. Love stings." It was odd, but I could feel the battle around me—a pulling to something or someone—and at the same time a pulling away.

Then a guy named Gordon grabbed my attention. I guess I liked him, but something else caught my eye. He acted differently—kind, not after just one thing. When he asked me to go to church with him, for the first time in a long time...I went.

I immediately felt something I hadn't experienced since I sang with the youth group. In that church was a love no man had ever shown me. It looked beyond the grown-up woman I'd become and straight into the heart of a broken little girl still inside. And then it spoke: "COME HOME."

And I did.

When I finally accepted God with an open heart, he filled a void—the need to be wanted, desired, and accepted. And I felt the yearning inside that drove me to search for answers finally subsiding. Somehow being in relationship with Christ took my insecurities away and filled me with contentment I'd never known before. As I grew in my relationship with Christ, I noticed for the first time I really cared about myself and wanted what was best for me.

So I made two hard—but right—decisions. The first one was not to get into a relationship with Gordon. For the first time in my life I didn't choose a relationship with a guy to make me feel whole. The other thing I decided was not to go back to the same college where I was known as a party girl. Some friends didn't understand why I had to live differently, and so a lot of "friendships" ended. But I never really felt that was a big loss because God became a *true* friend to me, there at any time, day or night. I felt God's presence surrounding me on good days and bad, and best of all I didn't have to surrender myself in ways I wasn't comfortable with to receive his love.

God's faithful companionship continued throughout the years, and he eventually made my heart whole again. Though it wasn't always easy, I waited for many years to enter into a serious relationship. It took a lot of prayers, crying, and leaning on friends, but I didn't have sex from the time I gave my body and heart to God until the man I married captured all of me on our wedding night.

Being married and knowing someone intimately, sexually, and emotionally is wonderful. But even then there's still no one like God.

"Amazing love. How can this be? That you, my king, would die for me?"

Laurie Vines

HE IS A GOD OF ANSWERS AND GUIDANCE.

"I will lead the blind by ways they have not known, along unfamiliar paths I will guide them; I will turn the darkness into light before them and make the rough places smooth. These are the things I will do; I will not forsake them."
—Isaiah 42:16

POINTLESS PRAYER

> *"Jesus looked at them and said, 'With man this is impossible, but not with God; all things are possible with God.'"*
>
> —Mark 10:27

"Last night Ella went home." A few days later I got another message: "Kara passed away last night." In two weeks both five-year-old Ella and nine-year-old Kara had died. I'd been one of the many desperately begging God to heal them from devouring cancer. The whole time I waited for God to snatch the disease away. Instead he took them to heaven, and it broke my heart.

When I received the second message, I went into the bathroom and sobbed. Something inside me died with Ella and Kara. Why had God let them die? I knew God could heal them. But lately he'd said no to all the big things. Had all my prayers been for nothing?

I never talked about it with anyone, and I would never have admitted it then, but over the summer I began to doubt prayer. I didn't think God could work miracles. I just didn't believe he would anymore. Praying for a miracle seemed futile.

207

HE IS A GOD OF ANSWERS AND GUIDANCE

Then various other difficulties and trials piled up, adding to my silent but growing belief that prayer was pointless when it concerned life-changing events. I soon concluded my prayers were meaningless. I even wondered if God cared when I did pray.

Those thoughts haunted me as I started my first year in college. They hung like weights around my neck. Devotions felt like a mechanical operation, and I did them because I was required to.

I felt stagnant.

At the beginning of October, Luna, a friend at college, came to my room. "We need to talk," she informed me.

"What's wrong?" I leaned back in my chair.

"You know my friend Sadie?" Luna looked at the floor, biting the inside of her cheek. "She's got cancer... brain cancer. It's malignant. It's the size of a golf ball and is on a nerve at the base of her head. It's too big and too delicate to remove. She probably won't make it past Christmas."

"Where is she now?" My mouth felt as if it were made of cotton. Sadie was just starting college. Her boyfriend had just proposed to her. She was just starting life!

"She's in the hospital. But she's going home soon. There's nothing the doctors can do." Luna looked up at me. "Will you pray?"

"Sure..." But I remembered Kara and Ella and secretly wondered what the point in praying was. I prayed really hard for them, and God said no. But as hard as that was, I couldn't tell Luna. I leaned forward, feeling like the world's biggest hypocrite. "Dear Father..." I closed my eyes. "We don't understand why this is happening, but please be with Sadie and her family. Please don't let Sadie suffer."

I wanted to ask God to heal her, but how could I ask for the impossible when I knew he'd say no? It was safer to ask God to be with her and work some small act in her life. I felt I'd just given up on God as I finished the prayer with a lame, "Please let them feel your presence. In Jesus' name, amen."

Luna opened her eyes, smiling. "Thanks. It means a lot to me. I know Sadie'd be thankful, too. And keep praying for her. She's the only Christian in her family."

As Luna left I felt sick. Why didn't God work miracles anymore? Why didn't he answer prayer like he used to in the Bible days? I wanted to believe it was possible. But the nagging doubt clinging to the back of my mind said God wouldn't work a miracle.

"Why don't you ask me to heal her?" I felt God ask me. But I didn't answer. I couldn't, not even in my mind.

Sadie stayed on my heart, and I prayed for her comfort and her family's salvation. But that was all I could manage. Still I felt as if God was chasing me. Every campus chapel service and church meeting was about trusting God, prayer, and asking. One Wednesday in chapel the breaking point came with a reading of Matthew 7:7-11: "Ask and it will be given to you...For everyone who asks receives...If you, then, though you are evil, know how to give good gifts to your children, how much more will your Father in heaven give good gifts to those who ask him!"

My mind went numb. The request pressed harder: "Ask me to heal her."

When I got back to my room, I set my Bible back on its shelf and huddled on the bed.

"Father, I want to believe you work miracles and will do the impossible. But I'm so afraid. It seems whenever I ask you to do something, the answer is no. I don't want to hear no again. I begged you to let Ella and Kara live! I've prayed for so many people, and you always say no! Father, I'm sorry. It just seems pointless. But please forgive me and help me pray. Father, please...heal Sadie. Take away the cancer. In Jesus' name, amen."

The words clung to my mouth. But I didn't feel quite as sick afterward. I couldn't pray for her healing every time, but I asked God to work that miracle several times. And each time my hope built.

Two weeks after Luna first told me, she helped me make sugar cookies. "How's Sadie doing?" I asked, hoping for good news.

"Not too good." Luna shrugged, stirring the frosting. "They don't think she'll live past Thanksgiving now."

I wanted to throw up. It was as if God were betraying me. God had told me to ask him to heal Sadie. And I had! But Sadie was still dying. I knew God had the right to decide whether he answered with a yes or a no, but I wanted to scream. What good were the prayers?

"Keep asking me to heal her."

It wasn't an option. It was a command. And I obeyed. But I felt as if I was mouthing the words. I didn't believe it could happen. Over the next week and a half Luna kept giving me updates. They were never good. Sadie was just waiting to die.

"Keep praying for her," Luna said each time I talked to her.

"Keep asking me to heal her," God said each time I started to pray for her.

The second week in November I still couldn't believe God would actually heal Sadie. But I still prayed. As I headed outside, I saw Luna coming down the leaf-strewn path. "Hey." I waved at her.

"Hey!" Luna waved her arms. "Guess what? Sadie's better! Only the top of the tumor is malignant. They're performing surgery this week." Luna launched into a long explanation of how Sadie's family had gone to a second doctor and discovered the cancer had shrunk and was now operable. But I only half heard her. My mind spun as I considered—maybe God had said yes; maybe he'd work a miracle and heal Sadie.

Several hours later I was still in awe. "Thank you, God," I whispered, leaning against the wall. "Thank you so much."

We continued to for pray Sadie right through her surgery and as she slowly recovered. Now several months later Sadie's doing great. She's planning on getting married next summer, and she's back in school.

And I have renewed faith God is still answering prayers and working miracles. Sometimes he says no, but that doesn't mean he always will. And just because God sometimes says no doesn't mean he doesn't want us to continue to lean on him and trust he can still do the impossible.

J. M. Butler

THE PROM DATE

"How gracious he will be when you cry for help! As soon as he hears, he will answer you."

—Isaiah 30:19

I was pretty excited when Travis, a quarterback on our high school football team, asked me to the prom.

We'd met at a postgame party one night. Later when we'd see each other in the hall between classes, he would always smile at me and say, "Hi." Then one day Travis came across the lunch room and sat down beside me. I discovered he had a quiet voice and a cute, playful sense of humor. That was the day he asked me to be his date for the senior prom.

With the prom only three weeks away, I had lots to do to get ready. It was going to be held at a superswanky country club in Beverly Hills, so I needed a knockout fancy dress to look like a million bucks. But I only had a few dollars saved from my part-time job. The more I looked, the more upset I got. The nice dresses were way out of my price range.

Then one day I came across the perfect dress. When I tried it on, it was everything I'd hoped for. The only problem was not only did it look expensive—it was. So I talked to my mom about it, and she agreed to help me pay for it if I'd take on extra chores for a couple of months.

Next I had to come up with some money to get my hair and nails done. But that worked out, too, when a neighbor who worked in a beauty salon offered to fix my hair in an updo and give me a French manicure in exchange for babysitting her kids. For the final touch my best friend, Joanie, loaned me a great pair of pink high-heeled shoes that fit fine when I put cotton balls in the toes.

On the big night Travis showed up at my door with a gorgeous purple orchid corsage. He was polite to my mom and sort of bowed to me when he opened the door to his red Chevy convertible so I could step inside. He even put the top up so the wind wouldn't mess up my hairdo. In his black tuxedo and bow tie Travis looked more handsome than ever.

We soon arrived at the beautiful country club, which I decided was the most elegant place I'd ever seen. I couldn't take my eyes off the crystal chandeliers, giant floral arrangements, and huge tables loaded with what looked like every kind of food on the planet.

The dance floor was huge and crowded with people I didn't know. Travis seemed to know everyone, but he only danced with me. When the band took a break for intermission, Travis suggested we walk outside and look at the golf course. I agreed even though my feet were starting to hurt.

As we walked past the parking lot, Travis said, "Let's stop at my car and get a blanket so we can sit on the grass."

I hoped we wouldn't be walking very far, but Travis wanted to show me a small lake on the other side of some trees. We walked a long time. Off in the distance I heard the band begin to play, and I told Travis we'd better head on back. He said it was only a little bit farther, and he really wanted to show me the lake. When we finally got there and saw the moonlight reflected on the water, I had to admit it was beautiful.

Travis spread the blanket on the grass and said, "I know your feet must be hurting. Kick off your shoes and let's just sit down here and rest a couple of minutes before we go back."

I was out of breath, and my feet were hurting so I said, "Okay. That sounds good to me."

As soon as we sat down, the moonlight seemed to go to Travis's head. First he leaned toward me and gave me a gentle kiss. But then he started getting way too physical. At first I tried to joke with him. I pushed him away and told him with a smile, "Hey, down boy! Don't get carried away."

But it was obvious Travis wasn't in a joking mood. He was acting very serious and intense. Then I realized he'd planned the whole scene and knew exactly how he wanted it to turn out. I admit for one split second I felt a romantic thrill, but I immediately came to my senses and told him to stop and that I wanted to go back to the dance.

I tried to shove him away so I could get to my feet, but he overpowered me and held me down. That's when I panicked. I tried to scream, but only a weird squeak came out of my mouth. I felt totally helpless. I'd made the decision not to have sex until I got married, but it looked as if I was going to be forced into it. I didn't have much of a chance against a football quarterback.

Suddenly, out of nowhere the words *I will never leave you or forsake you* popped into my head. In that desperate moment I realized my only defense was going to be prayer. Silently, I prayed, "God, help me!" Then without my realizing it, I heard my voice calling out, "Oh, God, please help me!"

What happened next was so amazing I'll never forget it.

Travis jumped up as if he'd been scalded with boiling water. His manner and attitude completely changed. He backed away and offered a hand to help me up to my feet, blurting out and repeating over and over, "Diana, I'm sorry. Please forgive me. I'm so sorry!"

Although God has answered prayer after prayer for me since that night, it was and still is by far the most immediate and obvious response to prayer I've ever received.

It's possible Travis had a religious background that played a part in keeping him from committing date rape. One way or the other, though, God showed up in the moment to straighten Travis out or to protect me, and whichever it was, I'll always be grateful for the way God answered when I called.

Diana L. James

IN THE CURRENT

"For this God is our God for ever and ever; he will be our guide even to the end."

—Psalm 48:14

Things were fine. We were comfortable. We were the worship leaders and assistant youth leaders at my dad's church—Hope Chapel South Shore in Waikiki. Taylor and I had just gotten married and moved into our new apartment across the street from the beach and our best friends. We bought our first puppy, Pinto, and we were both successful in our jobs. I was next in line for a manager position, and my wife was finishing up her aesthetician license at a salon. Because we both grew up on Oahu, our immediate families were always there to help us if we ever had a problem—a little money here, a borrowed car there, and dinners at least once a week.

I love music. I play bass guitar and sing in a Christian rock and punk band. We've played almost everywhere you can play on Oahu, all over the outer islands many times, and even in Texas. Recently, we had an opportunity to do a mini-tour in California. While we were there, we felt God tell us to leave home behind and move to California. At first the idea sounded great. *Anything for you, God—we'd move to Africa if you called us there.* Then reality kicked in.

Could we really leave our family, church, friends, warm water and weather, dog, new home, truck, and jobs behind? Move to a place we knew nothing about? Where would we live? Where would we work? What about a car? Money? What church would we attend? Who would rent our apartment? God told us what to do, and it was illogical.

More and more Taylor and I felt the urgency to leave Hawaii as soon as possible. The most difficult decision we made together was the first one...saying yes to God. After we said yes, God began confirming our decision through people, prayer, and even the church. Our friend, a flight attendant for United, blessed us with one-way "buddy passes" to fly standby whenever we wanted to leave. After prayer and much discussion we chose September 30 as our departure date (and found out the day after we got to California that all buddy passes were void as of October 1 due to airport security...we just made it). That gave us three weeks to pack up our lives, rent out our apartment, and say our good-byes.

The September 11 tragedy took place the day after we chose our departure date. Fear and doubt ran rampant between the two of us. We held on to God's promises and reassurances. Even the tragedy didn't change what God was saying to us. He was still in control. "Don't be afraid, for I am with you. Don't be discouraged, for I am your God. I will strengthen you and help you. I will hold you up with my victorious right hand" (Isaiah 41:10, NLT).

We left Oahu with three bags of clothes, a skateboard, and two guitars. We had no idea where we were going to sleep when we got to California. We felt God was saying, "Just go now; I'll take care of you." Our family dropped us off at the airport and handed us over to

God. The first two days in California seemed like years. For our first week we ended up staying in Huntington Beach and sleeping on different people's floors. A friend of ours had recently moved to Huntington from Hawaii, so she was able to help us out a lot. We walked aimlessly around Huntington Beach, not knowing what to do or where to go. We assumed the first logical step would be for us to find a place to rent. We started to look for an apartment in the Huntington area, but prices were way too high, and we didn't feel any peace about settling down just yet. We were homesick, confused, and totally dependent on God to show us what to do next.

Before we moved to California, Taylor had begun praying about enrolling in a school to complete her degree. Vanguard University was the school God led us to. One day we borrowed a friend's truck to check out the campus. While we were there, we found a great program for Taylor, and things began to fall into place. A woman named Sue helped Taylor get everything she needed to enroll that semester, which had started a month earlier. Before we knew it, Taylor had her first class the following Tuesday.

But we still had no home, no vehicle, and no job. It didn't seem logical to take care of school first, but it was the only thing we felt peace about. I'll never forget dropping Taylor off for her first day of class. I was hungry and tired. I just wanted to eat, but I knew I needed to walk Tay to class. Before her first class she needed to stop at Sue's office again to sign another form. I was standing there while Sue and Tay were talking, dreaming about Jack in the Box, when Sue turned to me and asked me what I was doing there. I paused and then muttered I was here to play music. She asked me again what I was doing there. I didn't say anything this time. I stood there and thought for a moment...I was blank. Then she said with a smirk, "You need to be *here*."

She began rambling on and on about this leadership and ministry class, the program, and the professor... I couldn't focus. *Me in school? Right now? No. I'm still hungry, it's a four-hour class, I'm terrified of school*—but I had a strange urge to sit in on that class. So I did and...God blew me away! The class was awesome. God was definitely up to something.

The next day we felt prompted by God to go back to Vanguard and see if getting me enrolled was even a possibility. We went straight to Sue. She was so excited. She told me how she felt God telling her I was supposed to be there. Another woman at school, Rhonda, confirmed Sue's feelings and told her she was feeling the same thing. I began to wonder myself. I gave this entire situation up to God. It was too overwhelming for me. I prayed that if this were God's will, everything would work out.

We left and came back to Vanguard the next day to hand in my application. The wheels were already in motion. Sue was doing everything she could to get me in. Now you have to understand I hadn't been in school for almost 10 years at that point. After high school I took a couple of classes at a community college in Hawaii, but I always had such a hard time. School was the last thing on my mind. It never even crossed my mind. It'd only been a few days since we moved to California, and my wife and I were enrolled at Vanguard University. This was our first encounter with God's logic—and we learned God likes to defy all logic.

And we still didn't have a place to live, a car to drive, or jobs. But we were on campus talking to Sue again when we heard a rumor of a married couple who was leaving their apartment at school housing. Another thing you have to understand is that a couple leaving in the middle of the year *does not happen*. Taylor and I were at the bottom of the waiting list for Vanguard's housing. But Taylor and Sue

prayed together while I finished talking to some people, and then we rushed over to the housing office.

We were accepted and told we could pick up the keys to our apartment in a few days...and got a 63 percent discount for starting late in the semester. We were freaking out. It was a miracle. It was obviously God's perfect timing. He was making a way out of no way and proving himself again to be our provider—because it was nothing we did. God was in control, and we were in the current of this stream of blessings he was creating one after the other.

Another day we were talking with Sue, and we remembered her telling us we had to meet a man named Brett, a high school youth pastor. We met him and instantly connected. He invited us to go down to Carlsbad with their high school leaders to plan out the next year of events for the kids. We accepted the invitation, hopped on a bus full of people we didn't know, and headed down to a place we knew nothing about. It was only our fourth day in California, and God totally led us to serve with Brett and our new church family. We were beginning to see God really wanted us to be there. Things were falling into place faster than we could keep up with them. We were soon helping out with the morning worship team and leading the Sunday night worship for the high school group. God is so awesome.

There are so many more ways God has revealed himself to us. He provided us with all the furniture in our apartment. People called us and asked if we wanted stuff like their sofas, beds, shelves, phones, and dishes. We were given a brand-new microwave, free meals, and even a free computer. God provided wet suits and surfboards for us, things we'd had to give away when we left Hawaii.

We still don't own a car, but God has provided cars through other people. Our neighbors have a third truck they let us borrow for a couple of months. Another friend of ours has been letting us use his Range Rover while he takes frequent trips to Hawaii, and another friend freely lends her truck anytime we need. God not only provides; he abundantly provides.

God also provided us with just enough money to be able to live—and even made a way for us to go to Texas for Thanksgiving and Hawaii for Christmas. The funny thing is we feel as if God is telling us to wait on getting jobs (another example of God's logic). We've both worked since we were 14, and not working is something totally new and different. It's actually really hard just to wait on God—to wake up every morning, lay our lives before him, and tell God we're willing to do anything he wants. We ask God to show us where he wants us to be. How to be completely empty of our wills—just to trust God to provide. To work only to be in the center of God's rest, love, and will.

The rest of the band has just moved over, and we've seen God provide in abundance for them as well. I believe we'll be playing music, but I now know I won't have to depend on us "making it" as a band anymore (that's God's job).

Given the way God has shown us his ability to provide and guide our lives in amazing ways, we trust God has a lot more in store for all of us. All we have to do is depend on him...the most exciting, thrilling lifestyle anyone could ever lead.

And the adventure continues.

Josh Nordgren

REDIRECTED

I grew up with a family that went to church on special occasions. I mean, we knew about Jesus and could all say the Lord's Prayer, but we didn't really connect with God.

When I was seven years old, my parents divorced, and my mother suddenly started going to church on a regular basis. The divorce was much worse on my dad. He instead turned to spiritualism, which included things like consulting tarot cards, having mediums contact spirits from the dead, and performing séances and various rituals. Some people he associated with even sacrificed small animals, thinking this would increase their personal power. Not only did my dad practice this religion, but some of his friends and many in his family were also into spiritualism.

I soon felt torn between my parents and their chosen religions. Seeking the approval and love of my dad was important to me, since he'd left me behind in the divorce, but as I lived with my mother, I also had a strong desire to keep peace with her. Being interested in spiritualism became a way for me to gain favor with my dad and strengthen our relationship. So as a young girl, I dedicated half my life to spiritualism and half my life to Christianity.

I have to admit, I became fascinated by the quick and easy answers spiritualism provided. When I did things like read tarot cards, I felt powerful and in control. I usually read into them exactly what I wanted to hear, and I liked getting what I believed to be insights about my future.

By contrast, being Christian meant I was a sinner and not perfect. I didn't like the idea of having to ask anyone for forgiveness. And no matter how I prayed, I never got any answers from God: He never told me what my future would hold, nor did he speak to me in any way I could recognize.

By the time I turned 16, I started to feel emptier than I ever had before. I tried to fill the emptiness with distractions like movies and boys—whatever I could to escape my feelings and get some attention or acceptance. When this didn't work, I began to feel very sad and like my life was meaningless.

Then my school started a new program enlisting high school students to talk with eighth graders about drugs, sexuality, and other issues they were facing. That's when I started noticing something different about some of the students with whom I volunteered. Although they had issues like everyone else, they seemed to have a different perspective on life and were generally less troubled and just happier than the rest of us. I soon discovered most of them belonged to the Christian club at school. That got my attention, although I never attended any of their meetings.

One day someone handed me a free New Testament booklet. I randomly opened it to Romans and began to read. I was especially drawn to verse 8:39: "Neither height nor depth, nor anything else in all creation, will be able to separate us from the love of God that is in Christ Jesus our Lord." It showed me a different side of God: He created us out of love and couldn't be, nor would he want to be, separated from us under any circumstances. I still had a deep sense of abandonment from my parents' divorce, and I'd transferred that to God. Even though I spent every other weekend with my dad, he wasn't there for all the most important moments in my life. The bottom line was: My own dad walked out, and I witnessed him leaving me behind. So if he could do that to me, why would the God of the universe care about me?

But the Romans verse gave me a sense of hope that I could find love and acceptance from God. Still, I was reluctant to give up my commitment to spiritualism. I went on like this, on and off between religions, until I was 18. I'd delved so deep into spiritualism I was very adept at reading tarot cards and had surrounded myself with all sorts of things related to the religion. So my heart remained torn for a long time.

Nevertheless, I finally felt I needed to pick one religion to be focused on and dedicate all my time to. I figured once I did this, maybe my life would feel less disjointed and more complete. I leaned strongly toward spiritualism.

About that time a friend of mine had just started going to church, and she asked me to come with her. Being a good friend, I didn't want to make her go alone. After all, church was full of stuffy people who only cared about looking good and helping others so they could receive recognition, right? No way was I going to let one of *them* pull the wool over her eyes. So I went with her, ready to keep her from harm.

Surprisingly, the room was full of young adults like us. There weren't any of the stuffy people I was expecting. People were wearing ripped jeans and T-shirts like me. They had their feet on the pews and were chewing gum. The band was playing some cool music with loud drums and electric guitars. I'm sure if my mother'd heard it, she would've freaked.

I ended up really liking the church; however, the rush of it wore off as the week went on, and the experience faded away. But my friend really wanted to check it out again the following week, so I agreed to go with her. As the band played, I started to think about how all of this was cool—except I still didn't really connect to it. People were worshiping God, and it seemed as if he was talking to them. I'd heard stories of God doing crazy things and giving signs to people, but I never noticed him trying to get my attention.

As I was thinking this, my heart began to beat, and I began to feel sad and desperate. I realized I longed to know God in a personal way. At that moment, standing in that pew, I decided I'd try to talk to God just this once and see if he'd answer me. My heart began calling out to him, and every word I said I actually meant with all of my soul. Quietly, I whispered so no one else could hear me, "God, I want to know you. I want you to use me to help others. Please answer me and help me."

As I said these words, I suddenly began to cry. Everything the world had taught me told me God wouldn't answer. I knew if this were true and he didn't respond, I'd leave him forever and cease to look at Christianity.

Suddenly, I stopped talking and began to listen to what was going on around me. It was very odd because the entire room had gone completely quiet. When I opened my eyes and looked up, a man had walked up on stage, taken the microphone from the lead singer, and

stopped the band. The singer seemed puzzled, but the two of them talked briefly, and then the singer moved back to give the man more room. The man spoke into the microphone, saying he had a message from God for a girl in the audience. And then the absolute weirdest thing happened. He began to describe this girl's life word for word. As he went on, I realized he was describing *my* life to a tee. He finished by saying he'd be sitting in the last pew in the left section and he'd like the girl to come and see him so he could give her the message. Then he left the stage, and the band started playing again.

My heart was beating even faster now. Everything that man said seemed to be pointing to me. My best friend, who knew me well enough to recognize he was speaking to me, was looking at me with awe. My first reaction was God would never talk to me—so this couldn't be for me. But I wanted to hope it was.

I decided I'd wait until most of the people were gone to see if anyone would go and see the man who'd spoken. When the service ended, I waited for a long time, but no one approached him. Finally, I got up the courage to grab my best friend's hand and dragged her with me to talk to him.

Although he didn't understand what the message for me was all about, he said he was supposed to tell me God was proud of me for turning away from spiritualism. Then he told me about a dream I'd had over and over for two years. In the dream I was called just to get up and leave everything behind, and then I'd be nailed to a cross and killed. I'd wake up, and my wrists would be sore where the nails would've gone in. My ribcage would ache, and I'd have a fever in the morning. The man said he was to let me know I'd incorrectly interpreted the dream. He told me many things—things he couldn't possibly know about me. When he was done, he asked if he could pray for me. As he was doing so, for the first time in my life I really felt God's presence. For the first time I understood God actually did care about me—he'd sent this man because God wanted me to know he was undeniably answering my prayer.

From that moment on I stopped being involved in spiritualism and turned all the way to God and his Son, Jesus Christ. Well, when I say I turned to God, I redirected my will toward him. I still had a hard time getting rid of my old tarot cards and things having to do with spiritualism because I was kind of reluctant to give up the personal power and access to answers spiritualism seemed to give. I'd invested thousands of dollars in the highest quality cards, expensive and even rare books, and special rings and bracelets associated with spiritualism. So a lot of nights I got mad at God or even sad because it was hard to separate from these things and the sentimentality they held in my life—including the connection to my dad all of this had given me. But God slowly brought me through it. I argued with him a lot, but over time I finally rid myself of these possessions.

By that time my dad was a high elder in his church of spiritualism, so he was in line to become pastor. When I told my dad my news about becoming a Christian, he tried everything to lure me back into spiritualism. He actually paid for a well-known medium to fly from London to Canada to try to convince me not to abandon my knowledge and dedication to spiritualism. He tried to tell me Christians were wrong and condemned spiritualism because they were just scared of what they didn't know.

As this went on, I called to Jesus over and over in my head. When this man tried to channel spirits for me, he couldn't get anything to come through. This actually made him really angry and frustrated. Finally, he and my dad insisted I spend the night in the church of spiritualism and sleep next to the altar. My dad stayed there with me, but it was still a very scary night. I don't remember if I

even slept. In the end my dad recognized I was serious about getting out of spiritualism and living a Christian life, so he finally gave up.

My life didn't become perfect overnight when I accepted Christ and denounced spiritualism; in a way it became more challenging. But I can't deny God's work in my life or the way he answers my prayers.

A few months after I turned to Christ, God miraculously provided thousands of dollars for me to go with a group to Scotland to work with youth in the poorest section of the country. The people there lived in extremely terrible conditions. We lived alongside rapists and drug dealers and tried to minister to anyone in the area. For nine months we served everyone from babies to the elderly in every way we could. Then God sent me to Madrid for outreach. I helped serve people there after the terrorist train bombings.

During that year God showed me far more crazy things than a total stranger who stopped a band to give me a message. I witnessed people healed and kids helped and hope reborn. More important, I saw Jesus, and this time I didn't run from him. You know, he can be crazy cool when you give him a chance.

It took me until after my year in Scotland and Spain to finally understand the proper interpretation of the recurring, painful dream I'd endured. It became clear to me: I *was* to pick up and leave—which I did—to go and do God's work. Dying on the cross symbolized my dying to myself to become what God wanted me to be. When I finally did these things, God gave me a new heart and strength. I'd always been a homebody who was terrified of flying off into the unknown. But God lifted me out of my fear. He also helped me see he'd been trying, through that dream, to give me a glimpse of what he had in store for my future.

One of the most powerful changes I witnessed came unexpectedly as I was in Scotland. I was sitting around, watching the movie *Braveheart,* when a phone call came through for me. It was my dad. He called to let me know he'd given up spiritualism and become a Christian. Just as he told me the news over the phone, Mel Gibson's character threw his sword up in the air and screamed, "Freedom!"

Knowing now that God does speak to us in all kinds of ways, I honestly don't think it was a coincidence.

Nicole Pipke

CLEARING THE WAY

—Psalm 18:36, CEV

Are you kidding me, God?

That question consumed my mind as an obstinate airline attendant stared at me, shaking her head. All I could do was look down in disbelief at my life neatly packed in eight U-Haul boxes at my feet.

I'd loaded all those boxes into the car, and my family and best friend, Jenny, had driven to Los Angeles International Airport to see me off. My friend who was coming along was checking in for our noon flight. I got to the front of the line to find out the name on my ticket was incorrect. There'd been a miscommunication between me and the missions department at my church, and I was denied access to board the plane.

After all the logistical, emotional, and spiritual preparations, I'd missed my flight and the chance to travel with a person I knew. I then learned I wouldn't be able to fly out until the following week.

I plopped down on one of the boxes and thought, *How can I say good-bye to everyone again? Do I unpack my precisely 70-pound bags to live for the next week?*

I woke up the next morning feeling as if my heart were in my stomach. But I had to cling to the fact I was depending on God—he was going to get me through this and into the mission to which he'd called me.

People generally have a hard time understanding things Christians are called to do for God. "You're going backward in life." That was my favorite comment.

I'd made a pact with God earlier in my college career. I'd wanted to be a travel journalist, but I told God if I followed his call and became a teacher, I'd really love to teach anywhere...in northern San Diego. I quickly realized my last year of school that the security of home and the 60-mile radius I'd mapped in my mind weren't going to be an immediate reality—God was calling me to be a missionary teacher in Malawi, Africa.

I went through every excuse I could think of to deny God's call. I rationalized that kids and people in my life in San Diego needed me. And I questioned what kind of daughter, granddaughter, niece, and friend I'd be if I moved. Lastly, I repeatedly told myself the profession of teaching is a mission field in and of itself.

But God was not influenced by my rationalizations. I had signs everywhere leading me to listen to him. Whenever I went to bed, the call to go to Africa was the last thing on my mind, and I'd wake up with a heavy heart. I quickly learned what happens when you're a child saying no to your heavenly Father due to fear of the unknown. I persistently said no for an embarrassing eight months. Running from God's call for all that time created a burdened, tired spirit in me—one I couldn't bear much longer.

One night after church I e-mailed the principal of the school in Malawi and told him I'd come the following term to fill the third-grade teaching position. The minute I hit "send," I was overjoyed with a peace I'd never known nor will ever forget. Although uncertainty lay ahead, and I was truly scared of the possibilities of the unknown, that spirit of heaviness was lifted, and I was suddenly filled with a longing to dance.

One of the biggest reasons I denied my calling for so long was pain at the thought of leaving my family and friends. The thought of telling my parents I'd be moving halfway around the world brought tears to my eyes. God knew, and his gentle hand lovingly cleared the way for the separation. Even though my family somberly accepted the news, I could tell they'd been given a divine understanding of what God wanted for me.

My friends cried when I told them I was moving, yet they were overwhelmingly happy to see and hear what God had in store. Even the supervisor of my credential program buried me in a hug when she found out, saying, "I'm so happy you're going to serve in a place where I know I'll go someday." From the time I said yes to God to the day I tried to board the plane, God provided encouragement through supportive people while building my character through people who didn't agree with my decision. God also built my trust in him through situations that had the potential to hinder my leaving.

Missing my flight was the icing on the cake of trials that'd come one after another once I'd committed to going.

Two months before I left, my car broke down, and the estimate for repairs was about a thousand dollars. I immediately panicked because I was in the midst of raising funds to go to Africa—which didn't leave room for a huge repair bill. But while I was waiting in the shop as they worked on my car, I was talking with the owner when my plans for the upcoming months came up in conversation. When the work was done and I received my bill, I was not charged for labor, and the bill was less than half the estimate. When I asked the mechanic about it, he told me, "Don't worry about it; you have bigger things to do." I was immediately reminded God is in every detail when we give our lives to him. That realization made me regret my worrying.

Apparently, God knew I needed further lessons in this area of trust, and I was soon challenged again when I went to the dentist for a routine cleaning. I got an awful surprise. I was informed two of my bridges were loose and needed to be replaced. If they weren't, my teeth could possibility rot, and I'd really be in trouble once in Africa. There was no way around it.

Unfortunately, I'd already changed to international health insurance, so I wasn't covered by dental insurance any longer. I meekly asked how much it would be to replace the bridges. The dentist looked at me and replied, "$6,000 for the pieces, plus labor."

I was speechless. Again I felt forced to begin trying to scheme ways to come up with that kind of money while asking people to support me. As I do when I rely on my own hands, I came up empty. I left the dental office and went to my mom's workplace. That's where I broke down.

I was physically tired of all the tangible preparations, spiritually tired from all the questioning I was receiving from disagreeing people, and emotionally tired from saying good-bye to those I loved. Now this! I felt as though I was running hard and going backward.

That night I cried out to God, saying, "You've called me to this mission. I've fought an internal battle with you

and external battles with others, but why must I continually come up against these situations? I can't handle it anymore. I want to quit, get a job here, and lead a 'normal life'!"

But God was once again refining me in subtle ways through his faithfulness.

The following week was filled with prayers, which were followed by incredible peace. I even found myself chuckling a little at the thought of having to make a 24-hour journey to come home on account of rotting teeth. A week after my appointment my dentist called to reveal he'd found faulty lab work on my present bridges, and as a result the bridges would have to be replaced free of charge!

God was clearing the way for what he was calling me to do. In things I viewed as catastrophic God showed his faithful guidance and love. He'd shown me he had plans for me far greater than the obstacles I encountered.

The extra week I had at home because of the mix-up with my ticket gave me the chance to enjoy my family awhile longer and to take a little trip with my mom. It gave me a chance to spend quality time with people I loved without being consumed by thoughts of packing and moving preparations.

God even blessed me on the flight by assigning me a seat next to a missionary who was my age and coming home after teaching for a year in China. She was full of excitement and advice for me. And with her presence came an audible voice from God saying, "You didn't get to travel with one of your fellow missionaries, but I have more!"

As I stare out my bedroom window at the amazing African sunset, I look back on those trials with a joyful

heart. I was able to experience how God moves for those who follow him, clearing the way, alleviating hindrances, and preparing every aspect of what he has planned. All we have to do is seek his voice and say yes, even through difficulties. I felt God's delight as he squelched hindrances and poured personalized and perfectly timed blessings on each situation.

My life here isn't easy, but I wouldn't forfeit my journey for any price or convenience.

I've been able to witness the true heart of the Father and as a result put the beat of my heart in sync with his. Seeing African culture and God's beautiful people and even acknowledging my culture shock—with an understanding that God goes before me and guides me in all circumstances—allow me to truly grasp a bit of God's plan for the world and most definitely his divine plan for me.

Haley Vile

A SNAPSHOT DIVINELY COMPOSED

"Every good and perfect gift is from above, coming down from the Father of the heavenly lights, who does not change like shifting shadows."

—James 1:17

People often view God as someone who undoes our messes, cures our anxieties, and tends to our requests. I would like to propose—yes, God does all of these things, but his motive for giving aid, for answering, and for guiding is for us to understand his love better. When asked, God is eager to make his love and aid more fully realized, even if it's accomplished through what we might call a very small occurrence.

This semester I'm in a photography class at college. I finally received my first real assignment after a couple weeks of classroom work and was thrilled go out on my own and shoot my first roll of film. I decided to shoot the film at home because there I'd have both a car and a big city at my disposal—two things I don't have at school.

I arrived in Indianapolis on a very windy and cold Saturday morning and was ready to begin shooting. I had my scenery picked out, my subject in place, and my lens in focus. The only thing I had left to do was adjust my camera's light settings. I pushed the shutter halfway down, but the light indicator didn't come on when I looked into my viewfinder. My light meter was broken, and I had no idea how to tell if I was taking my pictures correctly or not. I was extremely frustrated but nonetheless used my best estimations and took time to shoot the film anyway. After repairing my light meter that evening, I found out the settings I'd used for my film earlier that day were incorrect, so I knew I'd have no other choice but to reshoot before the weekend ended.

Sunday afternoon came quickly. I looked into my familiar bedroom and took a few steps toward my bed. As I did, my composure fled, and I dropped to my knees. The realization that I had to rethink and retake all of my pictures before I went back to school had been weighing heavily on my mind since the night before, but now the anxiety and reality of all of it set in. There I found myself stooped in front of my bed, my face buried into my sheets, beginning to think of the dozen other worries pressing on me that weekend. It was too much for me to handle. Tears came and remained in my closed eyes until they couldn't anymore. I wished more than anything I didn't have to go back out into the cold to start all over. The tears began to cover the sheets my face was pressed into. I lacked energy, focus, and motivation. With a weak and weary voice, I spoke, "Jesus, I just don't have it in me today to shoot this project all over again. Please—please help me. I need you to let me see your love today. Motivate me by your love."

I rose and left my house. I didn't have time to go to the city again, so I stayed nearer home this time. I drove down a nearby state road in hopes of finding a good side street where I could pull over and take pictures. After about 10 minutes of driving and searching, a particular moment came when I felt inclined, nudged even, to look to my left. My gaze went out past my closed window and

then immediately up to the sky, and I saw the sun shining so strikingly I lost my breath.

There were thick, dark clouds hovering in the gray winter sky. That dullness could have consumed the scene, but the sun was behind the clouds singing a song that couldn't be contained by clouds. The sun shone through the clouds with great strength in a distinct circle, and out from it burst forth rays just as bright in every direction. I pulled over as quickly as I could and jumped out of the car, camera around my neck—my breath still absent. Within seconds I adjusted my light settings and brought the camera to my eye. As I stood next to the car, eyes squinting at this splendor before me, I carefully turned my lens, and the image came into focus. I let my camera fall from my face, and it dropped back down around my neck. I couldn't help but just stare. This was majesty, and God had put it right in front of my face, almost posing for my picture. The idea I was going to have to settle for pictures that weren't as good was gone from my mind at that point.

As I brought the camera back up to my eyes, the piercing sun and those beautiful rays came through with clarity, and so did something else I hadn't even thought to include. Along the left side of the image, a telephone post stretched from bottom to top, while its cables traveled across the top, making a perfect frame around that striking ray-filled sky. *Nice touch, God,* I thought. I'd been considering the sunset great enough on its own to make the picture, but our imaginative God thought he'd make it better still. The picture I was seeing had been masterfully composed, and I hadn't done any of it.

Tears came for the second time that day, but these weren't the earlier tears of frustration in front of my bed. These were tears of overwhelming joy and wonder at how God had chosen to answer my prayer. That day I was tired, and perhaps what I expected of God was that he'd grant me the strength to go out and take the pictures. While he did supply strength, he did more than that. God led me to a place where I beheld a scene thoughtfully created so I could realize his love. It was interesting to think in that moment, the energy, focus, and motivation I'd lacked earlier came flooding into me all at once. The weight of frustration also nearly a day old left me in that moment. This was God's answer, his guidance, and his help; this was his love, but it hadn't come the way I expected. God is not weak or halfhearted, so when he loves, he loves truly, mightily, and without restraint—in a strong and whole way our minds don't initially understand. God put forth a flawless, divinely composed photograph, and his love stretched past that Sunday and was even plainly visible for the rest of the week. For example, when I developed my film on Monday, the negatives I had from the city on Saturday that shouldn't have turned out *did* turn out, and they were beautiful. In fact, many pictures from that particular roll of film ended up being used for the project.

I found my expectations of how God's love would be expressed were based on my own finite imagination. What we see around us in strangers, in our neighbors, and in ourselves every day is a sort of "half-love." It's what I find myself giving, what I see in our culture, and what I discover in our media. I found myself trying to guess how God might answer my prayer and show his love to me, but I couldn't. The love I'd envisioned God giving turned out to be a muted snapshot of the real love he was more than ready to lavish on me.

He's a God who loves from an unending wealth. God gives aid imaginatively and in plenty. God insists on answering our cries for help, and God guides the troubled and burdened. God answers when he's called on, and he pours out his love and aid in excess on those who simply ask.

Kellyn Walker

HE IS A GOD OF REFUGE AND COMFORT.

"The Lord is good, a refuge in times of trouble."
—Nahum 1:7

HOPE IN THE MOURNING

"Hope deferred makes the heart sick, but a longing fulfilled is a tree of life."

—Proverbs 13:12

I felt like someone was sucking the life out of me as I held back a flood of tears. Walking around in circles from shock, I tried telling myself these kinds of things only happen on television, not in real life to real people. I grasped for something familiar but found nothing. *What was I going to do? How would I go back to living?* My life had fallen apart.

It was Halloween—fitting day to begin living a nightmare. It was one of the coldest days I can ever remember, probably partially due to the uncontrollable chills running up and down my spine. There I was at the top of Dock A at a marina in the mountains of Colorado—where I was told my mom committed suicide.

After the memorial service six days later I returned home. The following week I was back at school. I went through the motions, but I felt dead. My life had been going along smoothly. I was a college freshman studying to become an emergency medical technician, was active in my church, and had a job I enjoyed. Considering every-

thing, my life was comfortable. But now I felt as if a part of me had died.

Out of desperation I'd find myself crying alone in my car, trying to hide my pain. Not letting others know what I was going through meant I didn't have to process it all or put out energy to help people understand what I'd been through. I'd been a transfer student coming into Colorado Christian University, so I didn't have anyone who knew about my mom or my pain or any of my personal history.

Finally, one night my pain and frustration burst through, and I cried out to God, letting him know how angry I was that he'd allowed this to happen. I told God I didn't see why I should trust him anymore. I knew it was my mom's choice, but still God allowed it. *Why?* I wanted to know.

After being a Christian for 11 years, I thought my faith was strong; my walk could handle anything. But now I found myself questioning whether God even existed. I couldn't fathom a God who'd allow a mother of six to kill herself. My heart was just shattered.

I spent the next couple of months trying my hardest to run from God. I kept going to church, but I stepped down from the worship team and the prayer team. Then I stopped going to the college group on a regular basis. I found I suddenly hated worship; it was so agonizing—it felt as if the God of all comfort had turned his face against me. Everyone kept telling me God was close to the brokenhearted, yet I felt he was nowhere to be found. I was hurting so badly, and I felt as if no one had any idea of the depth of my pain.

I finally came to a place of such misery I knew I had to make a decision. Was I going to allow my heart to become hardened toward God, or was I going to surrender? The weight of this crisis was slowly killing me, rotting me from the inside out.

The people in my life recognized how badly I was struggling, but they didn't know what to do. I could tell they hurt for me, and I know they held me up in prayer, yet no one knew what to say.

Then one Sunday a couple who were friends of mine from church gave me a CD. They told me one of the songs on it would encourage me. I reluctantly took it; I didn't see how a song was going to help. But later that day while driving, I decided to play the song. It was "Keep Singing" by Mercy Me. As I listened, I began to cry. The lyrics made me realize I could no longer carry this burden on my own—I had to surrender.

I cried out to God again, but this time I told him I was sorry for trying to handle everything myself. I needed God so much; I needed him to restore the joy I'd lost. I needed him to restore my hope for the future. I needed God to hold his devastated, scared, hurting child in his arms.

I asked God for help.

As soon as I prayed, I felt a huge weight lift from my shoulders, and a peace I can't explain came over me. At last I allowed myself to rest in the arms of my Savior.

Then God quietly spoke to my spirit, reassuring me I wasn't alone. And although my mom was not suddenly raised from the dead, my family was still a fractured mess, and my heart was still shattered, it felt remarkably good just to know I wasn't carrying this burden alone anymore. I knew there'd still be hard months ahead, but knowing God's love and help would be there to get me past the pain was the greatest realization in the world.

Aside from when I was at church, I'd felt alone most of the time. But after that day God in his ever-so-faithful way, knowing my heart better than I do, provided me with an amazing counselor on campus. Evidently, God orchestrated the entire relationship from the time we met till now. Not only was God faithful to provide me with someone who had the training to help me through the grief process, but he also provided an amazing young woman, Ashley, who's now one of my closest friends. In a matter of months we've come to feel as if we've known each other for years. We've developed a friendship that can only come from God. So in God's infinite wisdom, he met my needs.

Now it's been over a year, and things are still extremely hard. I never thought I'd go through something that would test my faith like the death of my mother. My heart still hurts every day. There's not a moment when I don't think about her. But even though I've been going through the darkest valley of my entire life, in the midst of all this I know God is meeting me. He's provided amazing people to walk beside me through the valley. He didn't make a way around it; he hasn't made it go away—he provided a way through it where there'd seemed no way.

While the pain is a present reminder of what happened, God is showing me he's ever so close, even if I can't feel him. He is there and will carry me as I trust him to lead me through this time.

Alie Aukerman

LOVE THAT HEALS

"People will...be proud, stuck-up, rude, and disobedient to their parents."

—2 Timothy 3:2, CEV

"I will heal you and love you without limit."

—Hosea 14:4, CEV

If you want to hear it straight, I thought he was a jerk.

There were five years between us, and my brother did his best to make my life as miserable as possible. He was tall, handsome, funny, and popular, and the girls who chose me as a friend didn't do so because I was anything special but because I was his sister. They wanted any opportunity to get near him. Little did they know, their very association with me annihilated their chances.

It all started because he was the baby before I came along. With three older brothers he got all the attention. And then this little girl came into the family five years later. Everyone was making a big fuss, and John's special spot was taken. I think that's what happened. Because the torture began about the moment I opened my eyes. We

grew and our fighting grew. He pinched me and laughed while I cried. He took my little boat, the one the Weebles used to play in, hung it from a tree on the other side of the brook, and shot little holes in it with his BB gun. He took Jason, my most treasured stuffed dog, and pounded him on whatever hard surface was in reach. In his eyes I was a crybaby and a brat. I was every name in every book. He pushed, he shoved, and he ignored.

And as I grew into my own, I played my own role. I pushed him to the edge, irritated him, and tattled on him. It wasn't good.

It didn't get much better when John went off to college. By then he'd earned the reputation of golden boy in our family. He was academically skilled, obedient at all the right times, and could make people laugh like nobody's business. But rather than celebrate his good fortune, I was upset about the whole thing. He smelled like a rose, but I'd lived with his thorns.

And then there was my life. I was quickly heading south. I began skipping school, smoking, hanging out with the rougher crowd. I was also lying...a lot. My parents couldn't trust me anymore.

My safe place was camp—a summer camp I attended every year. I had friends there, not like the people at school. The kids at camp loved me. Sure, they were a little different...mixed personalities who drank a ton of coffee and smoked up a storm, but they were home to me. I belonged there. None of them made fun of me—they didn't make me feel somehow less; they just loved me as I was.

It was around April when my mom threatened if I didn't quit smoking, I wouldn't be able to work at camp that summer. My boyfriend would be there, my friends would be there, my *life* would be there.

But I was also addicted to cigarettes.

One day I was sitting in my room, blowing smoke out of a small hole I'd placed in my screen. It was later in the evening; everyone was supposed to be downstairs. Suddenly, my mom opened the bedroom door and busted me. She called to my father in a wild, I-give-up kind of voice. She said in Dutch, her native language, "She's smoking!"

I knew right away what that meant for me: no camp.

My stomach dropped, and I immediately started crying. It was a harsh, broken cry. I couldn't imagine summer without camp. I couldn't imagine NOT being with my friends—my *only* friends. I cried harder.

Mom went downstairs in her anger, and I walked slowly down the hall, tears streaming down my face. John's bedroom door was open. He was home for spring break. He was sitting on his bed, and he waved me in. There was a look of tenderness on his face I'd never seen before. I sat beside him. He put his arm around me and pulled me close. "I'm so sorry," he said. Of course he'd heard the whole thing. "Does this mean you won't be able to go to camp?"

I nodded my head, feeling the sobs coming up again. "I'm so sorry," he said again. He sounded like he meant it. I raised my head and looked at him. He had tears in his eyes. "I wish I could do more." He paused as a single tear spilled over and down his cheek. "But all I can do is cry with you."

I couldn't believe it.

Even as I write this many years later, I feel the same awe I felt in that moment. My hardened brother had been

softened. We'd been raised in a Christian family, but his faith and love had become real while he was away at college. He'd grown to the point where he could look at his little sister, his once archrival, and love her in a sadness she herself had caused.

The look in his eyes melted me. My brother offered me grace and comfort when I messed up. The kindness of his heart touched me to the core. In that very moment my big, mean brother revealed to me God truly can change hearts. The evidence of God's work in him was undeniable and unforgettable.

As I continued down my wayward path, I hurt a lot of people. But never did I forget what my brother did—what *God* did in him. And as I grew older, there came a day when I cried and cried over my own poor choices. Because of John, I could almost imagine my Savior with a tear in his own eye, grieving with me. Not taking away the consequences but being my refuge and comfort as I faced them. God used the memory of that authentic glimpse of love, so unexpected and so miraculous, to remind me of his love and bring me home again.

Elsa Kok Colopy

LETTING GO

> *"You will keep in perfect peace him whose mind is steadfast, because he trusts in you. Trust in the Lord forever, for the Lord, the Lord, is the Rock eternal."*
>
> —Isaiah 26:3-4

Sometimes selfish desires get in the way of the truth. Sometimes they even block out God's plans.

As I watched my best friend pile into the car with her family and drive away, I was overwhelmed with selfish thoughts piercing straight through my heart like darts. My eyes filled with tears, and I silently cried as I watched the pale yellow car scoot along the street—out of my life. Thoughts of how unfair this whole thing was created a tug-of-war inside my head. I understood the reason she and her family had to leave. Still, logic argued with anger, which ultimately gave way to sorrow.

I'd known practically from the day I met her she wouldn't be in California for more than three years. Yet during our friendship we'd always labeled good-byes as "later," naively hoping the parting would never have to come at all. When did the time pass?

Mindy and her family were moving to Africa. *Africa!* The name still sends a chill through me. My inner eye sees the foreign country's wild animals and rough open spaces. Then I picture Mindy and the thin silver necklace she wears, symbolizing our friendship. How would she fit in?

A person closer than a sister was practically gone. I couldn't bring myself to wipe away a single tear. *I have a right to cry,* I thought. I also thought I had a right to be angry. My heart swelled with emotion as I traced our best memories. Why did all of that have to change? My life had been perfect. I couldn't understand why anything needed readjusting.

Later that day we made our way into the sunlight, which felt too bright and cheery for the kind of day I was having. As my mom started the car, the radio smoothly clicked on, and the tape I'd recorded began to play. Sound drummed through the speakers. My eyes closed as the words of my favorite Christian singer filled the car like a breath of fresh air. How many times had I heard it without listening? For at that moment the song had the exact words I needed to hear: "You know better than I...you know the way...I've let go the need to know why 'cause you know better than I."

At this amazing chorus a blanket of comfort and love surrounded my broken heart. More tears drizzled down my chin, and instead of stopping, I only cried harder. Suddenly, I knew how wrong my anger had been, and I began to pray, "God, I'm sorry. I'm sorry for not remembering you have a plan and a reason for all this. Comfort my best friend and me right now. You've called her family to spread your Word in Africa. I was wrong, and now I see how selfish my thoughts were. Give them courage to face the obstacles that will confront them."

I sighed and felt my bitterness slowly diminish. My heart still ached for the friend I wouldn't be seeing for a long time, but I was filled with quiet peace.

At that moment, out of nowhere, our cars pulled up next to each other at a red light. Mindy stuck her hand out the window and waved. I grinned softly and waved back. When her car turned a corner and we lost sight of each other, I knew everything would work out. God had a plan, and I was to trust and keep faith.

Mindy and I would never really need to say good-bye. We had many chapters to go in the story of our friendship. This next one was just taking us on separate adventures. We'd share the details of it all—*later.*

Kristina Marie Drummond

LOOK HOW THEY SHINE

> *"What a wonderful God we have—he is the Father of our Lord Jesus Christ, the source of every mercy, and the one who so wonderfully comforts and strengthens us in our hardships and trials. And why does he do this? So that when others are troubled, needing our sympathy and encouragement, we can pass on to them this same help and comfort God has given to us."*
>
> —2 Corinthians 1:3-4, LB

Our ragtag gang consisting of four senior citizens, one dentist, a couple of potential adoptive parents, a few "regular" people, and the four "kids" (my friends Kaitlyn, Ace, Joel, and me) landed in Moscow in the middle of the night. The happiest bunch of Russians you've ever seen promptly greeted us and stuffed our luggage inside the van they'd driven for three hours to collect us.

Once at the hotel we waited in the lobby as some of the men tried their best to open the van's back door. When their battle finally proved futile, they ended up just taking the whole back door off to get our luggage out. Nearly cross-eyed weary from traveling halfway across the world, we finally got our things and went to bed. The next

morning we all squeezed into the van again and headed for another city called Ryzan, which is about three hours south of Moscow.

When we got outside Moscow, we really had a chance to see the countryside. It was autumn, and everything was gold and red and bright and beautiful. I described it in a postcard to a friend as looking like Liberace's wardrobe had thrown up all over everything but in a really good way.

In Ryzan we got a chance to meet a lot of younger people from local churches. One night we were bombarded for two hours with questions about what it's like to live in America. After all the initial curiosities were settled, we asked a few questions about what it's like living in Russia. We learned there wasn't much opportunity, and a lot of the young people there had little hope. There aren't many jobs available, so most young people have no work. Many of the young girls turn to prostitution and the young men to alcoholism. Often young people who grow up in orphanages end up on drugs and in jail. Needless to say, hearing all of this broke our hearts.

Getting to know these people was wonderful, but it wasn't nearly as moving as encountering those whom we went to Russia to meet.

We visited nine orphanages, and at each one I was hard-pressed to find a face I didn't instantly fall in love with. It overwhelmed me to go from one to the next, only to find them all full of helpless, beautiful children. I couldn't and still can't wrap my brain around how there could be so many irresponsible people to account for so many discarded children.

The orphanages in Ryzan are set up based on learning level as well as physical ability. At one orphanage a lot of the older kids knew English pretty well. At another

the kids were placed there because they supposedly had lower learning levels, which I believe is just a result of not having a parent to read with them and expand their minds one-on-one. The kids never get the individual attention they need.

The next few orphanages we went to are the ones that really stick out in my mind. They were in a small town called Elichtma, which is three hours away from Ryzan, so we drove there one morning, spent the night at the only hotel in the town, and stayed most of the next day. We'd brought along a 17-year-old boy named Viktor who lived in an orphanage in Ryzan. We weren't quite sure why he'd come with us, but we didn't question it. Viktor knew English very well, so my friend Kaitlyn and I tried to get to know him and find out what it was like to have grown up in orphanages.

On our way there we'd stopped at a few small markets, and the men from the church bought huge boxes of bananas. After the kids finished their program, we gave them the bananas, and I just wish you could've seen the looks on their faces. Many of the kids came up and asked us to peel the bananas for them, and we discovered they didn't know how to open them because it was the first time they'd ever had bananas in their lives. I can't even tell you what it felt like to have given such a gift to these kids. I couldn't help but think of how many bananas have gone bad in my kitchen because I didn't feel like eating them.

After the kids had settled down and had their mouths full of sweet, mushy banana, one of the men from our group who'd been to these orphanages many times got up and began talking to the children about Viktor. Some of the men from our group and the church had made a visit to Elichtma a few months earlier and thought one of the boys looked like Viktor. When they asked him his last name, they found it was the same. Kaitlyn and I listened in astonishment as we found out Viktor had accompanied our group on our trip because he had a younger brother at this orphanage whom he hadn't seen in more than 10 years.

Viktor's younger brother had no idea his older brother was there to see him, and when they were reintroduced, it was a sight to behold. Both of them were crying and hugging each other and laughing. It was so wonderful to be part of their reunion.

The kids at this orphanage spent most of the day at school, and then every evening they walked a mile down the road to what was a jail when it was built in the late 1800s. Needless to say, there was a bit of an eerie feel to the place. The building had neither heating nor bathrooms. For toilets there were holes in the cement floors, and for bathing there were buckets to fill with cold water. The building smelled strongly of mildew, and it was rather disheartening to think this place was where the kids had to sleep every night.

The next day we visited an orphanage where the kids put on a fall festival, and we got to dance and sing with them. At one point we all held hands in a circle and walked and sang. As we did, I watched the little girl holding my left hand take her hand, pick and then wipe her nose with it, and then go back to clenching my hand again. There was nothing I could do but laugh. After the circle we sat down again, and an adorable little boy stood up by himself and sang us a song.

As he was singing away, I became overwhelmed. I suddenly thought of all the musicals and recitals I'd done as a little girl and how at every one of them I'd look out into the audience and see my parents and my family. I remembered how I'd sometimes peek from behind the curtain before the show to try to see where my family was sitting.

It hit me that this little boy and all these children would never know the feeling of singing and having their parents hear them. They'd never perform and afterward hear all their family members say what a wonderful job they'd done. They'd never get flowers from their aunts or chocolates from their grandmothers after their performances. I started to cry as I listened to this little boy sing his heart out for us, and I clapped as hard as I could when he finished.

The final orphanage we visited made the greatest impact on me. It was specifically for children with severe physical disabilities. Most of the children's grandparents were part of the Chernobyl incident, and the radiation had passed down through their genes and created deformities and severe medical conditions for the third generation of the people exposed. Many of these kids have neurological diseases and are severely mentally disabled, and others are deformed in ways Russian medicine can't yet deal with.

Our group went to visit the kids in hopes of comforting them. I tried to think of what I could possibly do for them, and I decided all I could give them was the gift I'd been given: my voice. Even if they couldn't understand it or even really hear it, I just wanted to sing to them the way their parents should've sung to them. I wanted to sing to them because I knew it was probably the only time anyone ever would.

As we entered their rooms, many of the people in our group were too timid to go to the children. For some reason God created me comfortable around people in such conditions. It was easy for me to see God in their little faces. I visited one boy who'd probably been in his bed for eight years. His big, bald head protruded from beneath his blanket where his frail body lay. His bony little arms led to hands missing fingers, and his eyes searched the room, never really fixing on any one object. I sat next to his bed and stroked his arm and face to give him some sort of stimulation, and as I did, I sang one of my favorite songs, the only one I could think to sing. It's been a favorite of mine for years, and at that moment it took on a completely new meaning. It's the song "Yellow" by the band Coldplay. Some of the lyrics are as follows:*

> Look at the stars,
> Look how they shine for you,
> And everything you do,
> Yeah, they were all yellow.
>
> Your skin
> Oh yeah, your skin and bones,
> Turn into something beautiful,
> You know
> You know I love you so,
> You know I love you so.

Then I sat there looking at his little body, this little bunch of skin and bones, and just told him how beautiful he was. And as I sang to him and stroked his arms, every so often I'd come across a ticklish place, and the boy would smile. At the sides of his smile were the two most beautiful dimples I've ever seen. His crooked smile was a thing of remarkable beauty crafted by a remarkable Creator.

While I'll never understand why people are sometimes born in these vegetable-like states and confined to their beds for their entire lives, and others are born in complete health and given incredible opportunities—I could look into that little boy's clear blue eyes and see the peace and comfort of God. Somehow as I tried my best to comfort him, he comforted me and my feelings of sorrow for him as he intermittently smiled.

* from the album *Parachutes*, 2000, EMI

And in that moment I realized God provides comfort and hope to people in so many ways: through his grace when people are unexplainably given a sense of peace and calm and even through people whom we see as hopeless and forgotten, who are hungry, sick, poor, and discouraged.

I believe the stars shine for them more than anyone.

Marleigh Dunlap

MINUTE BY MINUTE

"Who can forget the wonders he performs—
deeds of mercy and of grace?"

—Psalm 111:4, LB

Just like a crazy, random alarm, one ring after the next broke the early morning quiet. Saturday, I had enough clarity to remember. What on earth could be so urgent?

The morning fog swirling in my head slowed me down enough to figure out where the ringing phone was located—just as it stopped ringing. I moved on to find the next one: my cell phone, then my work cell. Finally, I caught a live phone and recognized the number as belonging to my brother. "What's up, Mikie?" I demanded.

"Jason's in the hospital, and it's bad," he informed me. "He might not make it." Those words alarmed me, but my natural defenses didn't let me immediately assume the worst. I figured he was probably in bad shape but would come around. As Mikie told me more about what'd happened, I gathered up my things, got myself dressed, and went out the door.

On the way to the hospital my other brother, Danny, called. Danny was Jason's age and a really good friend of

his, too. He was sobbing into the phone, but through his sobs I understood the tests showed Jason had no brain activity whatsoever. All hope was gone for our lifelong friend.

How could this be happening, God? I wanted to know. *Not Jason!* He'd never been in a better place in his life. Jason was always smiling, always taking time to plan things to do to get all of our friends together.

That Friday night he'd been with a group of his coworkers who'd taken him out to celebrate his recent promotion. Throughout the course of the night a couple of guys sitting near them kept hitting on a few of the single girls in his group. The girls didn't appreciate their advances, and Jason, in the spirit of trying to look out for them, casually walked over and let the guys know the girls weren't interested and asked them to stop harassing the girls.

It appears they didn't appreciate being told whom they could or couldn't hit on, and one of the guys shoved Jason. He fell backward, hitting his head on the floor. The impact caused his brain to swell and cut off his oxygen, and that killed his brain.

The only bright spot in this nightmare was that Jason's family, knowing it was what Jason would've wanted, donated seven of his organs to people waiting to receive them. A 16-year-old would receive his heart. To make that happen, Jason would remain on life support until Sunday at 6 p.m.

But even with the knowledge this had been arranged, the shock of it all was so severe and surreal it was really hard to believe Jason was truly gone.

As the reality of it began to set in, a big group of Jason's best friends got together to find photos of Jason for his memorial. That's when we noticed a weird phenomenon. Several of the photos taken of Jason in recent months had these strange bursts of light glowing around Jason's head. It made us wonder if God hadn't been preparing him for his pending journey. Sometimes when you lose someone you love so tragically and suddenly, you look for things that help bring comfort. In their own weird way those photos validated that Jason really was someone special.

Sunday afternoon dragged by with the feeling a wet, heavy blanket was draped over me. The sadness was too much to bear. I just wanted to sleep so I wouldn't have to face reality. My heart was heavy, and I was in sore shape, in definite need of some sort of refuge. But I remembered at 6 p.m., Jason was going to be taken off life support, so to honor the moment they'd officially end the prolonging of Jason's life, I stepped into my living room to sit with my family and say a prayer for him.

I looked at the clock at 5:59. Just as I was sitting down, without anyone touching the set or remote control, the television turned off. It'd never done that before. We all looked at each other, but instead of trying to come up with a reason, we went on with the prayer and prayed steadily for Jason for the next few minutes. I said the last words, telling Jason how much we all loved him and would miss him. Then I looked up at the clock. It was 6:03. I bowed my head and said, "Amen." Just as I finished, the television turned back on. Again no one had touched it. Seriously.

A deep sense of awe came over me and again an unexplainable comfort.

I know God is all-powerful and his mercy knows no end. I choose to believe God's power and grace cleared the way for a sincere, uninterrupted prayer to be said to usher Jason into heaven. When Jason was safely there

and our prayers were done, God put things back the way they'd been. With the noise of life buzzing around us, life was our gift for at least another minute.

And that's how I'm dealing with my grief: minute by minute sometimes, hour by hour at other times. God's gift of time does have a way of healing our hearts. But time also has a way, through our memories, of never letting us forget the gifts he's given us—gifts like Jason.

Ryan Fischer

ENDURING THE UNENDURABLE

"We pray that you'll have the strength to stick it out over the long haul—not the grim strength of gritting your teeth but the glory-strength God gives. It is strength that endures the unendurable and spills over into joy, thanking the Father who makes us strong enough to take part in everything bright and beautiful that he has for us."

—Colossians 1:11-12, *The Message*

I found that promise in God's Word when I was sitting on the edge of a hospital bed, waiting to be brought up to the operating room for what was supposed to be a relatively straightforward surgery and recovery process. Had I known the significance of the verses, I would've gotten up and run out of the hospital. But I really had no way of knowing what was about to come my way.

Waking up after surgery, I got the first hint something was wrong in the form of unbearable pain. Having had the same operation done to remove a cyst almost two years earlier to the day, I knew this wasn't the same as last time, and it turned out I was right. Later I found out the cyst was very large and wrapped around many organs, making its removal very difficult. And as a result

of its size, the incision ended up being twice the size of the previous one, so the pain was intense to say the least.

I went home from the hospital four days later, and at first things seemed fine. Day by day I was regaining mobility, and the pain was decreasing. The drain they'd put in after surgery was removed, and the incision itself was beginning to heal.

Then the real "adventure" began.

It started with a fever, and then my body began to shake uncontrollably. If that wasn't enough, the little hole left from the drain turned into Niagara Falls, and out flowed a liquid that looked a lot like blood. Panicked, my mom rushed me to the hospital where they did some testing and found I had a blood clot. I was sent home with some antibiotics and a promise things would get better in a few days' time.

But they didn't get better; in fact, they got worse. My energy level dropped to the point where I spent most of my time in bed and couldn't stay awake long enough even to watch television. The fever continued, and my body was ravaged by shakes. Then my skin went completely white, and my lips started turning blue, so back to the hospital I went.

After I was admitted, the doctor on duty decided to run more tests and start an IV. Within minutes I had one guy looking to find a vein in my left arm to take blood and a nurse looking to start an IV in the other. Here I was sick as a dog, with people fishing for veins in both arms. I had bright lights in my face and felt like my head was on fire from the fever. And the only thought crossing my mind was, *Why?*

Why, God, are you allowing this? Wasn't what I've been through already enough? How come my prayers haven't been answered? Why won't you heal me?

As I cried out to God, a sense of peace came over me, but at the time it honestly wasn't good enough. I wanted answers but wasn't getting any. All the while I kept praying for God to make me well. I couldn't understand what was wrong with me or why this was happening, but I did know God had the power to stop it—and he didn't.

That was hard to swallow.

I spent that night in the hospital and after waking up in the morning was sent home with more antibiotics and the assurance things would be fine. But again things weren't fine. I continued to get worse until finally on another trip to the emergency room, a specialist was called in. After taking one look at my incision, he said, "You've got an infection, and we've got to operate." He then went on to explain they'd reopen the incision, remove the blood clot, pack the wound, and leave it open to close on its own over the next few months.

Normally, the thought of walking around with an open wound would freak me right out, but the peace of God came over me, and an hour later I was in surgery again.

Over the next 10 days in the hospital the struggle continued as my body tried to fight a major infection and weakness caused by both surgeries, among other things. But in the midst of all the struggles and the pain and the sickness I found strength not my own. In reality I didn't know how things were going to turn out, but this unexplainable source of strength brought me through what was humanly unendurable. And this very strength reminded me I wasn't alone. This strength was also accompanied

HE IS A GOD OF REFUGE AND COMFORT

by peace. And in that peace I felt comforted and even reassured.

Several antibiotics and another surgery later I still had an infection that wasn't going away and no guarantee it would. But even in the midst of the infection I knew whatever happened, it was going to be okay. Somewhere throughout my battle with sickness, any issues I had about the sovereignty of God were settled, and I knew he was in control.

Finally, almost three weeks after the first surgery things began to improve. My white blood cell count returned to normal, and the fever stopped, so the doctors decided to let me go home. My house has never looked so appealing.

But the "adventure" wasn't over yet. For the next six months I faced a difficult recovery battling further infections and experiencing the unpleasantness that comes with having an open wound needing to be packed (and unpacked) every day. But it was okay because I learned no matter what came my way, God was with me—and he truly does give us strength to endure even what seems unendurable. As one e-mail I got said: "Faith doesn't get you around trouble, but it does get you through it." Being a Christian didn't mean I was immune to any of the side effects of living in a fallen world, but it did mean I didn't have to face those side effects alone.

I don't think I'll ever understand why God allowed so many cysts to grow in my body or why he didn't heal the infection the moment it surfaced, but I do know I'll never forget the power of his presence and the comfort God gave me in the midst of pain and sickness. And I'm truly thankful for that.

God encourages us to lay our troubles at his feet and let him carry our load: "For you are weak, but I am

strong." (1 Corinthians 4:10) God allowed me access to the strength and peace only he can give, which makes no human sense when you experience it in the midst of troubling times.

Kristen McNulty

ON THE TRAIL

> *"Though I walk in the midst of trouble, you preserve my life."*
>
> —Psalm 138:7

It was a Monday morning, and I woke up feeling spiritually stuck and just kind of dried up in my faith. For the past weeks, months—well, I guess really, the past year—I'd been fighting with myself and God about where I was and where I was going.

Most of my spiritual apathy was coming from a place of bitterness. I'd been resenting God over the direction he was taking me. I felt unworthy of the responsibility he'd placed on me, which involved other people's growth or lack thereof in their relationships with God. I often questioned whether God had the right guy and whether he was really big enough to make up for what I'm not.

I felt so lethargic I actually had a soft drink for breakfast. I was just totally out of it. By 11 o'clock I realized if I didn't get out and do something, I was going to waste the day watching TV or doing nothing at all. I also recognized I could use some time with God to try to sort out why I was so spiritually funky. So I decided to go on a hike on a trail close to my house, one I hiked often while growing up.

As I opened the door to leave, I thought I probably ought to take my Bible along. I didn't really want the extra weight to hike with. But then I thought I might feel guilty for not bringing it, so I grabbed my backpack, put a water bottle and my Bible in it, and took off for the hiking trail.

I arrived at the back entrance of the park. One of the first things I usually saw at that entrance was a trickling little creek. This day the creek was flooded from recent rains in what turned out to be one of the rainiest seasons for the area in years. I made my way up to the trail head and began the hike, distracted already by thoughts of the world and a bunch of things I didn't want to think about. So I stopped and prayed and asked God to refocus my thoughts on him. I walked a little bit farther, and the same thing happened again. This time I stopped, closed my eyes, and took a deep breath—and when I did, I got this very crisp, clear mental picture. The only way I can think to describe it would be dirt with another layer of dirt flying over it. It was the weirdest picture. I don't usually believe in visions and that sort of thing—I'm a skeptic. But then I got this tingly feeling, like when I hear someone speaking a message and I know the words are meant for me. So I said, "Okay, God, I have no idea what two layers of dirt have to do with me, but I'm open. Go ahead and do whatever you want to do with this heart."

Going on, I hiked on to a place in the trail where a big sign shows different snakes found in the park. I thought about how I hadn't seen a rattlesnake in the area since I was about 10 years old. Then this thought came into my head: *I don't think I'm going to see a rattlesnake today. I think I'm going to see a mountain lion.* I immediately thought, *That's crazy. I've never in my entire life heard of anyone seeing a mountain lion along this trail.* But I felt so strongly I

was going to see one, I picked up a rock about the size of my fist for each hand. If anything jumped out at me, I was going to smash it.

So I was hiking along with my backpack with a water bottle and my Bible in it and rocks in each hand, and the trail began to have a lot of loose dirt on it. I started to slip a lot and couldn't really brace myself with the rocks in my hands. So I got very symbolic for a moment and reasoned the rocks were much like some of the defenses I've built up in my life. I needed to let God just work in me, and although I admit the analogy seemed kind of cheesy and corny, it made sense to me. So I threw the rocks into the dirt. Although I was pretty far along the trail, probably about two miles out from any house, I began to relax and start to focus on the beauty around me, especially all of the greenery as a result of all the rain we'd had. Just a ton of flowers were out, some which I'd never seen before. I noticed there were six different flowers, and I picked one of each. Now I was holding three flowers in each hand instead of a big rock.

I reached a part of the trail where it came to a sharp incline leading briefly to a plateau and then continued with a steep downhill portion about 50 feet in length. I ran down one of the declines, and as I was coming back up another incline, I saw the hindquarters of an animal about the size of a German shepherd move into the bushes in front of me. I started to wonder if a dog was lost, and if so, I wanted to try to help it. Then I realized it was unlikely a dog would be this far out along the trail. But I decided whatever it was, I was going to find out. So I took a few more steps, and as I came around the bend, about 20 feet away a mountain lion was just sitting on the trail, staring me right in the eyes. I looked at it, and my brain still hadn't registered what it was. It looked like my cat, only bigger. I just stared at this animal, completely confused as to what it was because I'd never seen anything like it before. *Could it be a bobcat?* I wondered. But then I realized it was too big to be a bobcat. *I guess it could be a mountain lion,* I decided.

The funny part is I wasn't scared. I was more annoyed at the inconvenience of this imposing animal because I didn't want to end my hike yet. So I began wondering if there was any proper etiquette for passing a mountain lion on the trail. *If I kind of shuffle across facing him, would he let me go, or are there going to be some problems here?* I realized I probably didn't want to get any closer to this guy because he was pretty big. After about a minute I began backing up along the trail until I was pretty sure he wasn't coming after me. Then I turned and hiked out of the area. As I got nearer to where I was parked, I stopped for a minute to think about things.

That's when it registered in my brain that I'd just encountered a mountain lion. Just as I had that thought, the vision I'd seen in my mind earlier instantly came back. I saw that the top layer of dirt matched the coat of the mountain lion, and it was as though I was seeing it from above as it was running along the trail. That made sense to me, but I wondered exactly what any of it meant. I had no clue.

When I got home, I called to report I'd seen a mountain lion along the trail. "Really? What park were you in again?" the ranger asked.

I told him again, and he replied, "That's interesting. We closed that park. It's been closed for about 72 hours due to flooding. Did you come in the back entrance?"

When I told him I had, he said the closure had been posted at the front entrance. He also said with the absence of humans in the park, a lot of big-game wildlife like deer and mountain lions that wouldn't normally be there had been coming back.

Then he said, "Are you sure you saw a mountain lion? Can you describe it for me?" So I told him it looked like a big cat with a round face like a lion's but only a bit sleeker. Then he said, "Yep. You saw a mountain lion. You're lucky to be telling me about it."

After we hung up, I went online to look up information about survival techniques when encountering mountain lions and learned there are only a few tips because you don't usually encounter one unless it's attacking you. And if one attacks you, it's not too likely you survive.

The first thing they say to do is to keep eye contact with them, which I did. Another is to bulk up—wear a backpack, which I wasn't planning on doing, but did because I'd decided to bring my Bible. Another tip was to make sure you stand up straight and puff your chest out. Well, I'd just come running up a hill when I came across the mountain lion, so I was already doing that as I stopped and regrouped to get oxygen. And the last thing they tell you to do is make sure you have rocks to throw at it so it doesn't think you're an easy target. But I'd been standing 20 feet from a mountain lion, holding six flowers in my hands. I'd dropped my rocks and trusted God was there to protect me.

That point made me realize that in the end, no matter what, God is worth trusting. It also affirmed that both the direction of my life and the way it'll end are up to God.

The hike never ends. The trail continues to be a challenge. I still struggle and wonder. But I'm comforted in a weird way every time I think back to that day because I know now God really does have everything handled.

And that gets me through another day.

Tom Beigle

HE IS A GOD WITH A POWERFUL PRESENCE

"I can never escape from your spirit! I can never get away from your presence! If I go up to heaven, you are there; if I go down to the place of the dead, you are there. If I ride the wings of the morning, if I dwell by the farthest oceans, even there your hand will guide me, and your strength will support me."
—Psalm 139:7–10, NLT

STILL CONNECTED

> *"So we fix our eyes not on what is seen, but on what is unseen. For what is seen is temporary, but what is unseen is eternal."*
>
> —2 Corinthians 4:18

She was dying.

The silence of death pervaded the room where my grandmother Mama lay, slipping in and out of consciousness. At 91 her heart had given up, and she was tired of this world.

The muted sounds of the people working at the care center drifted to me as I sat alone by her bedside. The world was slipping away from her as she faced the doorway to eternal life. Even I could sense how distant the old world seemed to her as she turned her eyes toward her heavenly home.

How could I live without this woman who was more than a grandmother to me? How would I survive without her encouragement, her advice, her unconditional love, and her support? She and I were connected in some mysterious way—more than relatives and more than friends.

We knew each other's thoughts almost before we thought them ourselves.

Memories fluttered around my mind like butterflies in a rose garden. My mind's eye returned to my earliest memories—to her farmhouse, which had been her mother's before her and was now my house. I remembered the smells of Christmas as we gathered around the cedar tree my grandfather had perched in a bucket of water in the corner. There we sang carols, opened presents, and ate homemade candy. I remembered the noisy conversations of extended family dinners as aunts, uncles, and cousins joined around the large dining room table for fresh country-fried chicken, mounds of mashed potatoes, and chocolate pie with high, peaked meringue. I felt her arms holding me in the night as I snuggled close to her in the feather bed in the unheated upstairs bedroom. I laughed out loud as I remembered her disgust upon discovering me in my tree house smoking a cigarette I'd pawned from a boy at church.

Yes, she was more than a grandmother—more than a friend. She taught me about love and sacrifice. She taught me about faith in Jesus. Even though I'd moved around throughout my childhood, visits to my grandparents and to the little country church had given me roots and sustained and strengthened my faith. I glanced around the small room that had been Mama's recent home and noticed again the signs reminding me her faith had remained strong. Her Bible, worn with daily use, lay on her desk where she always sat reading it as I came in to visit. The plate with the picture of the Rising Sun Baptist Church hung on the wall, providing her a glimpse of the place of worship she'd attended since birth—the place I'd attended since birth.

I caught a movement on the bed and rose to lean over Mama as I always did. Her hearing was poor and her

eyesight dim with years, and I wanted her to know she wasn't alone. Her eyes fluttered open.

"I'm here, Mama. I love you." I spoke loudly and smiled grandly even though my heart was wringing with my grief. Feebly, she reached up to pat my cheek gently as she always did.

"I'm so glad to see you. You are so sweet. I love you, too." Her voice was so weak I could hardly hear her, but my heart heard her loud and clear.

I knew I had to let her go. When she had the stroke six years earlier, I'd prayed hard: "God, I'm not ready to let her go yet. I need her! You *can't* take her."

I got my way. God left Mama here, but she remained an invalid, paralyzed on her right side and unable to engage in her active life of gardening, cooking, and sewing for my family. I knew she'd been left for me—because I was too selfish to let her go.

I couldn't be that selfish again.

I sat down again watching her, memories fluttering around my mind. I searched for a way to gain spiritual strength. *Oh, Mama, if only you could help me strengthen my faith now*, I cried in my heart.

And then, as if she'd read my thoughts as she'd done all my life, she opened her eyes. Wide-eyed and with an unusual strength in her left arm, she reached up into the air where my face had just recently bent over her. I watched her pat the air and say, "Jesus, I'm so glad to see you. You are so sweet. I love you, too."

And I saw clearly (in my mind's eye) what she saw: Jesus bending over her, saying, "Elizabeth, I'm here. I love you."

Suddenly, her arm dropped, her eyes closed, and the room was again silent: silent but not the same. The room was brighter, the silence peaceful, my spirit calm. My faith was strengthened, and I knew she and Jesus had let me see exactly what I needed to see to let her go.

Soon my parents joined me around the bed. I climbed into the bed and held Mama in my arms as she made her way out of the chains of this life and into the freedom of her new life in heaven.

I could finally let her go because I knew she wasn't alone. Jesus was there to bridge the gap between this world and the next. Now she holds one of his hands, and I hold the other.

We're still connected.

Susan Rae Burns

STREAMS OF MERCY

"I have said these things to you, that in me you may have peace. In the world you will have tribulation. But take heart; I have over-come the world."

—John 16:33, ESV

Like many Christians, I was born in a Christian family, baptized and dedicated in the church, and grew up in a pretty rosy world. Neither I nor any of my family had any horrible sickness or condition. The only funeral I ever remember going to was my great-grandmother's—she died at 98. And in this secure environment the need for God didn't seem to exist, though I called myself a Christian and said I loved Jesus.

By the time I was a teenager my life had become very different from my childhood. Thanks to my growing indifference to Christ, I was slipping slowly and easily into sin—slight things at first. Nothing major. But soon I was regularly becoming disrespectful of my family, I fought with my brother, and I thought nothing of lying or any other "little" sin.

Then things got serious. I faltered and stumbled into lust through the Internet and through my increasingly

vivid imagination. My mind became consumed by lust, and it troubled me greatly. Part of me thought, *What have I become? Am I a Christian?* And another part soothingly answered, *There's nothing wrong. No one sees or cares. It's totally normal.*

I'd begun going down the wide and easy path and started to turn my back on God. Still, in this little secure life of mine, he didn't turn his back on me. God spoke to me in my pastor's sermons. He tried to make me lean on him and not on my own notion of strength and security. Events began to occur where later it became obvious God was shouting, "See? Trust me! Everything can break, except me!"

But I didn't listen.

When my grandparents divorced and we also learned my father had hepatitis C, I didn't lean on Christ. Instead I plunged headlong into sin, thoughtless of my future or faith.

Satan knew all of this. He knew I was weak and sinful. He knew I was taking myself down a dangerous road. He knew I was susceptible. He began to plague me with doubts, and my entire world started to crack and splinter along the edges. Doubts crowded the parts of my mind sin didn't take over. I began to dwell on them, think about them, and constantly wrestle with them. I woke up often in the black of night, utterly distressed.

Finally, my world ceased cracking and just broke completely.

One seemingly normal night my father, whom I idolized, announced he was leaving us. He simply gathered up his stuff and walked out the door. It seemed to me he was gathering up his life. I was stunned. I couldn't think, I couldn't cry, and I *certainly* wasn't about to pray.

In the months to follow I soon made up for my lack of emotion that night. I was filled with bitterness, anguish, anger, and hatred. My mind was swimming so hard with these emotions as my father left and found another life, another house, and a girlfriend that I finally, cautiously, reached for my Bible, which I'd left unread for many years. Painfully, I croaked a doubting prayer asking God for help. Then I randomly flipped to a certain page, half expecting to hear the words of God rip the sky open.

They didn't.

I became enraged at God and threw my Bible against the wall. I cried and screamed at him, "WHY? Do you care? Do you even see?" Satan, whose falsely comforting voice had become familiar in my ear answered, "Of course not. Your family doesn't care, and your friends don't care. *God* certainly doesn't care."

From that point on I lost my faith. Either God didn't exist, or he simply didn't care. The last light in my world seemed to flicker and die.

Not long after that a mysterious change came over my mother and brother. They began to read the Bible, prayed often, and talked about restoration and God working everything out. Inside I scoffed at them. *Working it out? Yeah, right,* I thought.

But strangest of all a sense of peace began to settle over my brother and mom. I didn't care at the time. My attitude was, *If they think God is real and can fix their lives, then let them.*

Finally, I hit my lowest point.

I'd witnessed my dad acting as if life was all great. I'd seen my friends, secure in their world. I'd heard my pastor talk of God, yet he and others at the church never

seemed to ask me what was going on or if I even thought God cared. My emotions all met and clashed right as I was having a huge fight with my mom. On edge, emotionally bleeding, and confused, I went in my room to be by myself.

I wasn't by myself. Satan was talking again.

"You're worthless. Your father is never coming back, and life will never, never get better," he lied. He continued to talk me down a path of failure with his lies.

"Your friends, your family, and your church don't care. They might even be glad you're gone." And in my state of confused pain I bought it. I was tired of life and of pain, and I didn't see an end anytime soon. I wanted to stop.

Numbly, I reached for a pad of paper and a pencil and quickly jotted down a suicide note. I was going to end it right then and there. Right as I was going to hang myself, the thought I expected to run through my mind was, *No one will care. Do it!* But a voice I hadn't heard or listened to in a long time talked to me in my pain.

It was Christ.

In the stillness of my thoughts I heard him gently say to me, "My son, *I* am here and *I* care."

I knew this was Christ. He seemed so compelling, convicting, and yet merciful. It gave a new meaning to the words "streams of mercy never ceasing" from an old hymn I'd often heard while growing up but never really related to.

I immediately let go of the rope, and since that night I've never let go of Christ. I know now God made it clear to me he always "works it out," and in all things he's already won the fight.

I can't say my life has turned around completely, but I now know one thing for sure. I could never deny God's grace, and I'll never forget having the privilege of being in his powerful presence.

Joe Laughon

GOD COMES TO HISTORY

"Be firm in your faith. Stay brave and strong."

—1 Corinthians 16:13, CEV

It was not the most exciting week in my life. I had just finished my U.S. history midterm and was looking forward to the weekend. Even the easiest teachers were hard on you when it came to talking while tests were still out. But my history teacher was especially strict about this rule, which made what was about to happen an even more mind-boggling experience.

He never let anyone talk in class, and as my desk was right in front of his, there was never a time when I could get away with talking, especially during a test.

Taylor sat one seat diagonally behind me. Now he can be a nice guy at times, but he was the one who ridiculed me most for my beliefs, especially when I brought my Bible to school. Then there was Byron who sat two seats over, a popular punk rocker and skinhead who claimed to love the devil and Satan-worshiping songs.

Taylor finished his exam and got up to turn it in. On his way back to his seat, as I was doodling on a piece of paper, he picked up my Bible. Normally, I would've been

TRUE VOL.2

very worried, wondering what he was going to do. He hadn't exactly been a fan of my Bible since school started. But for some strange reason that day I was comfortable with it. I thought it was because we'd gotten to know each other better the past two months and had even helped each other on some assignments.

After a few minutes I looked back at Taylor, and he was actually reading the Bible! I smiled at him, turned back around, and continued doodling. Exams were still out so I wasn't going to say a word, but God had another plan. Taylor passed me a note asking, "What is the verse about the Devil being loosed from his prison at the end of the thousand years?"

Now this completely amazed me. To my knowledge Taylor'd never read a Bible in his life. Stunned, I turned around and looked at him. "Can you find it for me?" he asked.

I'd never seen him so interested in something so I told him I'd try. I really didn't have any idea where that verse was other than probably in Revelation. So I prayed, "God, please let me find the verse he's looking for. He hasn't ever wanted to hear your Word so badly."

I opened to Revelation, and right under my right thumb was the title "The Thousand Years." I'd opened right to it. I immediately looked up and whispered, "Thank you, Jesus," half laughing out of joy and the feeling God was all around me. I turned to Taylor and handed him the Bible, open to the passage. I will never forget the look on his face when he asked me, "How'd you do that?" and I told him about my prayer.

Remember, we were talking out loud to each other, and the teacher seemed not to hear us. Maybe a little "divine intervention" perhaps?

HE IS A GOD WITH A POWERFUL PRESENCE

So Taylor read the story and then handed the Bible to Byron, who also read the story, as well as several more chapters in Revelation. While Byron was reading, I asked Taylor where he'd heard about "the thousand years." It was pretty wild to hear him tell me he'd seen it in a dream. I asked him what he got out of the story, and he said it was "kinda freaky." I told him Revelation could be a really strange book sometimes, and it's mainly about when Jesus comes back. The look I saw on his face told me he actually believed and maybe even got scared at the thought of Jesus coming back. He handed the Bible back, saying he could relate to some verses he'd read, and he wanted me to show him some more so he could read them.

So we spent 40 minutes just reading different verses. Taylor read some of them out loud to Ian, the guy who sat next to him and behind me, and finally gave my Bible back.

Right about that time the last test was turned in, and we were allowed to change seats and talk. At that point Taylor told Byron he didn't like the Devil anymore and was bored with the whole Devil thing. Then a few of Taylor's friends called him over to the other side of the room, and Taylor passed by my desk, grabbing my Bible on his way over. For the last 10 minutes of class Taylor read various verses out loud to about eight or 10 people on that side of the room until the bell rang.

In that moment I felt so much peace and joy—as if nothing could go wrong and nothing could hurt me. I've never felt so alive in my life and never felt the presence of God so strongly. It was as if he was sitting in the empty desk beside me. And to think people believe God isn't in our public schools and doesn't work in them. Half the class was exposed to the Bible that day, and five people heard me when I explained I'd prayed to find the verse and that was how I'd landed right on it.

I see evil every single day of my life, and I see so many non-Christian peers whose fates I worry about. That experience showed me how much of an impact one little action, like just bringing my Bible to school, can have.

God had given Taylor a dream about a verse that made him want to know more about the Bible. And God had used me to show Taylor where to find that verse.

Is God present in our everyday lives? I'd say so.

Casey Day

PLAYING BY THE RULES

> *"I treasure your word above all else; it keeps me from sinning against you."*
>
> —Psalm 119:11, CEV

My 10 Rules for High School

1. Get with a more popular crowd.

2. Dress in style.

3. Know about everything going on in the entertainment world.

4. Get a boyfriend.

5. Stay away from people I grew up with (a.k.a., uncool crowd).

6. Get with a more popular crowd.

7. Get out of going to church (although I've had to go every Sunday of my life since before I remember).

8. Keep believing in God; quit worrying at night about what will happen if I die.

9. Fit in with a more popular crowd.

10. Have some new adventures.

Addendum: Pass all of my classes.

For a long time I'd had a feeling things couldn't go on the way they were. I wasn't unhappy with my lifestyle; I just knew it was wrong but wouldn't admit it. Other, more important things were on my mind—like fitting in. Fitting in brought the biggest problems. The things I did were sort of fun, but I always knew deep down inside they weren't the real me. I truly fit with the chess club, for example, but having set out on the quest to fit in with a more popular group, there was no going back.

My friends from before didn't want me after I "sullied" myself with the new crowd. The new crowd would make fun of me if I hung out with the old crowd, and the tiny bit of popularity I'd gained would go down the tubes.

10 New Rules for High School—Midterm

1. Stay with the quest.

2. Remember the reward is worth the everyday effort even if I'm exhausted from it.

3. Jump into each new opportunity (close eyes if necessary).

4. Do not get left in the limbo of not fitting in anywhere.

5. Do what others are doing even if I don't want to.

6. Remember, drugs are only an experiment. (I'm not a druggie, for Pete's sake.)

7. Take what's offered.

8. Enjoy it.

9. Tell conscience to shut up.

10. Pass some of my classes.

One night I somehow ended up in a car with a friend between two guys in the front seat and me between two in the back seat. I only knew one of the guys, not so well, but when he offered a pill, I took it. Before long I was in another place—a crazy place—not a nice one. The other people in the car took the same drug but went to a happy place.

The other girl noticed something wasn't right.

"Are you okay?"

I sort of nodded my head yes and no at the same time. I couldn't talk.

The purveyor of pills kept looking at me with concern.

"This doesn't usually affect people the way it's affecting you."

Someone turned up the volume on the car stereo. Music and lyrics resounded through my confused mind like a racquetball bouncing off the walls of a court. Something was wrong, even fearful, about what I was hearing, but I couldn't figure it out. Everyone and everything faded except the music, yet I couldn't seem to understand a word.

My friend came into focus.

"Are you sure you're all right?"

"I guess so."

Then her face changed. It began to melt and ooze down toward her neck. The flesh ran until it dripped off her chin, leaving her eyes set in huge, empty sockets.

"What's wrong?" Concern shot into her voice.

I shook my head in the negative. The guys continued to talk and laugh about how great the drug was. My friend finally turned away. I leaned back and closed my eyes to shut out the picture.

How I wanted out of that car—safe and secure back at home. But I was wedged between two guys and unable to say a word. I doubt my body would've moved had I been able to speak or get out.

The music seemed to get louder. Maybe it did—I don't know—maybe it just got louder in my head. The song was about the fear of dying. The words "hang on to your life" played over and over. Terror engulfed me. Suddenly, the weird lyrics and music stopped, and the lead singer began to speak:

They gaped upon me with their mouths,
As a ravening and a roaring lion.
I am poured out like water,
And all my bones are out of joint:
My heart is like wax;
It is melted in the midst of my bowels.
My strength is dried up like a potsherd;

And my tongue cleaveth to my jaws;
And thou hast brought me into the dust of death.
    (Psalm 22:13-15, KJV)

What is happening? my mind screamed. *That's from the Bible! That's about Jesus on the cross! That doesn't belong here—not at this time, in this place. Am I really hearing it, or is it the drug?*

No one else said anything about the words, but they pierced my mind and heart over and over. Jesus hanging on the cross. Jesus suffering. Jesus' heart melted like wax—like my friend's face.

Oh, God, I'm so sorry I'm sitting here, doing this, and listening to the Bible at the same time, I cried out in my heart.

The misery didn't end in a second. It took awhile to be able to get coherent enough to go home, but my drug use stopped there. God's Word, no matter how or by whom it is presented, is still his Word.

New Rule for High School

1. Throw my rules away.

Sandra Holmes McGarrity

THE RICHER ONES

> *"Has not God chosen those who are poor in the eyes of the world to be rich in faith and to inherit the kingdom he promised those who love him?"*
>
> —James 2:5

The day I met him, I was in a hurry as always. I was running late for work and thinking about all the homework I had to do when I got home. As usual my thoughts revolved around me and only me.

He wasn't standing on a street corner as the homeless usually are, asking for money. He just stood there in front of the Burger King with a sign asking for food or donations.

I've always heard never to give money to homeless people because they're all bums and got that way from drug abuse or laziness. I'm sure some of them do—but not all, I learned.

He seemed sincerely to need food, so I made a quick decision to help him. Surely that wouldn't take too long, and I was already late anyway. So I told him to meet me inside and I'd buy him a meal.

He ordered a Whopper with large fries and a Dr Pepper. I ordered chicken nuggets. We sat down at the same table, and I decided to ask him about himself.

"So what are you doing out here?" I asked.

He didn't answer. I didn't blame him. But I had to try again.

"What's your name?" I asked.

This time it worked.

"James," he mumbled.

James. James no-last-name, the homeless man for whom I just bought a meal and was now even later to work.

"Well, James," I continued, "I don't have much time because I have to get to work, but I hope you enjoyed the meal."

He didn't let me go that easily, though.

"What's your name?" he asked.

"Jessica."

"Jessica is a really pretty name. It was my daughter's name."

My heart hurt at the *was* in his statement. I didn't want to ask what happened, and I'm glad I didn't. I realize how much pain other people go through.

"I bet your daughter was beautiful," I said and meant it.

He thanked me and asked if I come by this way very often. "Why yes, I do," I found myself saying. And before I knew it, we'd set a time to meet each week and share an early lunch.

Over the weeks I learned a lot from James. I learned about his ex-wife Patricia and their precious little daughter, Jessica. I learned how he lost Jessica in a tragic accident and how their loss tore James and Patricia apart. He doesn't even know where Patricia is anymore, but he's sure she's alive. He says husbands and wives are connected like that. He'd know if she weren't alive.

It took me at least a few months before I worked up the courage to take James to church with me. Big events like this never go as planned, kind of like weddings. Someone always forgets their role, forgets the ring. I warned all of my youth group friends to be on their best behavior and treat him well, treat him normally. "That's all he wants," I'd said, and I just knew they understood.

But my faith was weakened, and I almost left the church for good that day when my friends laughed at James's brown trousers with holes, well-worn and unwashed, and made fun of his haircut—or rather the haircut he didn't have. Yes, he was wild, but James was also my friend. He hurt and I hurt for him.

How could these people of God who I respected—my peers, my friends, my accountability partners—be so cruel? I wondered.

Then I realized I didn't see as much of God in action through the people I practiced my faith with as I did in this homeless man. The presence of God shone right through James in a powerful way and gave me greater insight into the way I think Christ would see things.

James explained I must forgive my friends.

"Sometimes," he said, "people do things they'll regret later, even much later, and regret is somethin' powerful. You just need to forgive."

I always thought before I met James that I had to go out of town, out of the country even, to be a missionary and impact the world. I thought I'd change the world, one third-world country at a time, with mission campaigns. I still support mission campaigns, and I still go on them, but now I push local outreach more. I help out with a local church's downtown ministry. We go to the slums of the city and hand out paper sacks with lunches and blankets. Through this ministry I regularly meet people who live at shelters until they're kicked out. Then they're back on the streets. I know a woman who lives in an old blue Chevy truck. The windows are broken, and the only blankets she has are ones we've given her.

When I left for college, I missed my weekly meetings with James. He doesn't have a phone, so I can't call him, but I go by and visit when I'm home for breaks. I tell James about the people I meet. I thought he'd like to know there are more people out there like him, but he never fails to amaze me. He sympathizes with the people. He thinks they're worse off than he is. He's a selfless man like that.

A lot of people ask me as I approach graduation what I plan to do with my life. People ask about graduate school or overseas mission programs or the work force. No one expects to hear I want to work at a shelter and help homeless people, but no one has the nerve to criticize it, either. Who can? It's a noble, sacrificial cause, they think, because they don't know yet that homeless people are people, too—people with less than they have, yet very often with far more faith.

I've come to believe people with a heart like James' are actually the richer ones.

Jessica Dunagan

WHAT A RIDE

> *"Go now to your countrymen in exile and speak to them. Say to them, 'This is what the Sovereign Lord says,' whether they listen or fail to listen."*

—Ezekiel 3:11

When I was in high school, I lived in central California where I met my friend J. J. He was a lot like the rest of us guys, except he was a Christian. He was just as much fun and crazy as any of my friends, but he didn't drink or party like we did. He'd still come and hang out with us; he just wouldn't do the kinds of things we did.

I moved a few hours away with my dad and sister after high school. It was a miserable situation because we just didn't seem to have any connection with each other. It was as if everyone were living separate lives under the same roof and didn't really care how or what the others were doing. My sister and I were constantly at each other's throats—taking out our stress on each other. Loving relationships had never exactly been modeled in our house. My mom drank heavily and left us when I was only 11. My dad was not much more of a role model, hiding behind his work, moving us into crazy situations.

At 19 I realized I needed to get something going for myself because my parents weren't likely to be much help. So I started studying music at a community college and was obsessed with it. I'd basically spend all day long practicing piano and upright bass.

But often on weekends I'd go and stay with J. J. and his family. I'd known them for years, and recently, his entire family had started going to church just like J. J. I was impressed by the way they'd become closer and more loving to each other. I knew they couldn't be putting on an act or faking the changes I saw. There was so much more love between them, more than I even remembered, and I wanted to get to the source of it. I wanted that kind of love in my life.

One night I went to a church meeting with J. J. and opened my heart to God. Nothing miraculous happened, but within a few weeks of accepting Jesus, I made the radical decision to drop out of school, move to J. J.'s and totally immerse myself in learning everything I could about God. The Bible came alive to me, and I began spending all my time reading, praying, and going to church.

After about six months it was time for me to get out of their house and go back to my life. So a bunch of friends got together to say good-bye and pray for me. While we were having this prayer meeting, one of my friends piped up in the middle of the whole thing and said, "God just showed me you're going to lead a broken, hurting family of seven to him." That's exactly what he said to me. And as crazy and off-the-wall as it sounded, we were all so focused on God moving in our lives that it seemed like a normal thing to say. I just took it like, "All right. Thanks for the message, bro."

After I moved back home, I forgot all about what he'd said. I was more focused on figuring out what God wanted me to do with my life.

One morning, a couple of months after I'd moved home, I planned to check out a new church I'd heard about. So I borrowed my dad's car and stopped to get some coffee on the way. I grabbed my favorite blend and was sitting in the car, sipping my coffee when I very distinctly felt God "speaking" to me. It wasn't like I heard clear sentences in my head, but more like I had overwhelming feelings and felt drawn, as if God was leading me on a journey and taking over my morning. I felt compelled just to start driving. It seemed so supernatural, and it was obvious to me God was there directing me, giving me this sense of which way to go moment to moment, step by step. It was very clear and very real, and I felt absolutely certain God was in charge and I was part of a plan.

I drove farther and farther away from home without a clue as to where I—or I should say we—were headed. But I felt incredibly close to God in the moment, and I just wanted to stay with him.

Every off-ramp became a prayerful decision, and soon I was nearly out of gas and realized I'd spent my last few dollars on coffee. So I thought to myself, *What are you doing, dude? You're aimlessly driving down the road to who-knows-where. How's this ever going to end up looking good for you?*

But just as I'd think doubt-filled thoughts, I'd sense God asking me if I trusted him. The way he was talking to me was so much of a miracle I had to go along with his plan.

I eventually ended up in a town in the next county over in a church parking lot. I asked God what the plan was now and sensed him telling me just to start walking. Pretty soon I passed a couple of Mormon guys talking to a guy on a corner. We exchanged hellos, but I didn't feel as though I was supposed to stop and talk with them. So I kept walking until I came upon a house where a couple

of guys who looked about my age were hanging out in front. It felt right to walk up and start talking to them, but they looked at me like, "Who do you think you are?" Since it was Sunday, I asked if they'd been to church, and they said they were going to go, but their car had broken down. I offered to come back and give them a ride to a later service, but they seemed as if they wanted me out of their face more than they wanted a ride to church.

So I decided to cruise around and see if there was a church in the neighborhood with a service later that day. A few blocks down the road a guy pulled up in a car. It turned out to be the same guy who'd been talking to the Mormons. We struck up a conversation and figured out we were both Christians. I told him how God had me on this journey and I didn't know what it was all about. I hadn't said a word to him about being nearly out of gas or anything when he said God had put it on his heart to give me some money. So he handed me 10 bucks, and right then I knew God had called this guy to be part of this journey.

On the way back to the car I passed by the house where the two guys had been, but there was only a young boy of about four or five years old out front. It seemed odd he was playing out there all alone. So I asked him where his family was, and he said his dad was in prison, his mom wasn't around much, and his three older brothers had gone to get beer. I asked if anyone else in his family was home, and he said his sister was inside by herself. Four brothers, a sister, and two parents: a family of seven. A broken family of seven! Until this conversation I didn't have a clue what God had been up to, but when I realized there were seven people in this family, I knew exactly why I was there.

Finally, the boy's brothers showed up, and when they saw I was back, they looked really annoyed. I figured I might get hurt, so I told them I'd checked out a church in the neighborhood that started at five o'clock and asked if I could still give them a ride. But they blew me off. I figured I wasn't making any progress with them, so I left to get some gas and try to find out what God would have me do next.

I found a gas station and went to put the 10 bucks in the tank, but as I was about to put the pump nozzle in, I felt God tell me to put only five bucks in and more specifically, to buy a package of KOOL cigarettes and some Hot Tamales® with the rest. I was like, "All right, God."

I felt I was supposed to go back and give the brothers the stuff I bought, but once I got there, I sat in the car frozen with fear. I didn't think I'd get away with invading their space again without getting worked over. But I realized my fear was intimidating me not to do what God was calling me to do. So I reached for my Bible and opened up to Isaiah. As soon as I began reading, it was as if God was using the Scripture to talk to me about this family—about the struggles they were going through and how there'd been a lot of fighting, brokenness, and dysfunction. I was suddenly overcome with a heavy heart for them, which was definitely from God because I could never just out of the blue have been burdened with such compassion for strangers.

As I continued reading, I felt God telling me he wanted me to convey a message to them to stop feuding and pull together as a family. So then fortified by God's Word and relating to them given my own family background, I was like, "Okay, let's do it." I stepped out of the car and went up to the door.

The little girl opened the door and called to the oldest brother who, when he saw who it was, quickly slammed the door in my face. So I stood there for a minute before I decided to try again. The girl opened the door, and this time I showed her the candy and cigarettes. She called

to the oldest brother, and he came toward me with this threatening, intimidating look, so I quickly blurted, "Look, all I know is God took over my day and led me all the way here to share something with you." I started just sharing God's heart with him. I hardly recall the details, but I remember telling him God saw their fighting and how it was tearing the family apart. God wanted them to know he's the Father of the fatherless and he loved them. I told him there's nothing God won't forgive. Then he agreed to let me pray for them.

When I finished praying, I noticed his attitude toward me had totally changed. He appeared thankful and no longer felt threatened.

I sensed I'd done what God had brought me there to do, so I said good-bye and got back in the car. I wondered if I'd finally arrived at the end of this journey, and in that moment I felt like a kid asking the age-old question, "Are we there yet?" But God wasn't done. I felt him compelling me to drive in the opposite direction from home. So I was like, *Okay, let the party keep rumbling.*

I wound up picking up a young kid who was hitchhiking. I wasn't given to picking up hitchhikers, but I felt God telling me to pull over and let him in. The car was now on fumes, but I drove into the local mountains as I listened to his story and talked to him about Jesus and church. That seemed like all I was supposed to do, so when we reached his destination, I turned around for home. But now I was way up in the mountains, and the car was flat out of gas. *What are you going to do about this one?* I silently asked God. The question had barely left my mind when I heard God tell me to pull over and look in the trunk. He said there was money in the pocket of a coat in there. No kidding. Clear as a bell, this is what I heard.

I pulled over, opened the trunk, and found my dad's raincoat, and sure enough, in one of the pockets I found a 20 dollar bill. I stood there clutching the 20, smiling up at the heavens and laughing out loud.

I found a gas station and grabbed some gas and a sandwich. I was suddenly starving and realized I hadn't eaten all day.

About an hour later I arrived back home. It was now nighttime, and I admit I was scared my dad was gonna kill me for taking his car and not even calling to let him know where I'd been. But when I got home, I found he'd been sick in bed all day, so he hadn't needed his car and didn't say a word about it.

God had led me by his very presence to fulfill a prophesy given to me by a friend months back, and I didn't have the faith to realize he'd worked out every detail right down to my dad's condition that day. I smiled at the thought of what it would be like to live every day in God's perfect will: to follow his lead, certain he always has the perfect master plan.

That night the words *what a ride* took on a new meaning.

Alistair Merryman

AFTERWORD

AFTERWORD

> *"My purpose in writing is to encourage you and assure you that the grace of God is with you no matter what happens."*

—1 Peter 5:12, NLT

> *"For I am convinced that neither death nor life, neither angels nor demons, neither the present nor the future, nor any powers, neither height nor depth, nor anything else in all creation, will be able to separate us from the love of God that is in Christ Jesus our Lord."*

—Romans 8:38-39

> *"I pray that from his glorious, unlimited resources he will give you mighty inner strength through his Holy Spirit. And I pray that Christ will be more and more at home in your hearts as you trust in him. May your roots go down deep into the soil of God's marvelous love. And may you have the power to understand, as all God's people should, how wide, how long, how high, and how*

deep his love really is. May you experience the love of Christ, though it is so great you will never fully understand it. Then you will be filled with the fullness of life and power that comes from God."

—Ephesians 3:16-19, NLT

GOT A GREAT GOD STORY?

We'd like to consider it for publication in *True Vol. 3*.

E-mail your story or story lead to true@lifewriters.com or send it snail mail to this address:

> True Vol. 3
> P.O. Box 10879
> Costa Mesa, CA 92627

If you'd like to read and help us select the stories to be included in *True Vol. 3*, e-mail us at truereaders@lifewriters.com.

GIVING BACK

To try to make a difference in the lives of teens and young adults beyond those who have an opportunity to read this book, a portion of the proceeds from the sale of this book will be donated to the Center for Student Missions (CSM).

CSM gives young people and adults the opportunity to live out the call to be Jesus' hands and feet to the poor and needy in North America's inner cities. CSM provides students with an effective urban ministry experience by participating in efforts such as rehabilitating apartments for low-income residents; serving food to and building relationships with hungry men, women, and children at soup kitchens and homeless shelters; planning and conducting weekend and weeklong backyard Bible clubs for inner-city children; joining inmates for worship and Bible study in prison chapel services; delivering meals to impoverished shut-ins; joining street-savvy urban Christians in evangelistic outreach in their local neighborhoods; and much more.

CSM offers mission trips to Chicago, Houston, Los Angeles, Nashville, New York, Philadelphia, San Francisco, Toronto, and Washington, D.C.

The Center for Student Missions
P.O. Box 900
Dana Point, CA 92629

Tel.: 949-248-8200
csm@csm.org
www.csm.org

IRENE DUNLAP

Irene Dunlap began her writing career in elementary school when she discovered her love for creating poetry, a passion she believes she inherited from her paternal grandmother. She expressed her love for words through writing fictional short stories and lyrics, as a participant in speech competitions, and eventually as a vocalist.

When Irene asked God to direct her to difference-making work that would leverage the talents and gifts she'd both acquired and been blessed with, he answered. She soon began working on *Chicken Soup for the Soul®* books, helping cocreate *Chicken Soup for the Kid's Soul*, *Chicken Soup for the Kid's Soul 2*, *Chicken Soup for the Preteen Soul*, *Chicken Soup for the Preteen Soul 2*, *Chicken Soup for the Soul Christmas Treasury for Kids*, and *Chicken Soup for the Girl's Soul*.

Irene believes her work with *Chicken Soup for the Soul* was the perfect preparation for creating the *True* book series, through which she hopes to reveal God's true character to teens and young adults. *True Vol. 1: Real Stories about God Showing Up in the Lives of Teens* was released in 2004.

During her college years, Irene traveled around the world on the Semester at Sea program aboard a ship that

served as a classroom and home base for more than 500 college students. After earning a bachelor of arts degree in communications, she became media director of Irvine Meadows Amphitheatre in Irvine, California. She went on to co-own an advertising and public relations agency specializing in entertainment and health care clients.

Irene continues to carry on a singing career, performing various styles of music but specializing in jazz. Irene lives in Newport Beach, California, with her husband, Kent; daughter Marleigh; son Weston; and Australian shepherd Gracie. In her spare time Irene enjoys horseback riding, gardening, traveling, entertaining, painting, and cooking. If you're wondering how she does it all, she'll refer you to her life verse for her answer: "Now glory be to God who by his mighty power at work within us is able to do far more than we would ever dare to ask or even dream of—infinitely beyond our highest prayers, desires, thoughts or hopes" (Ephesians 3:20, LB).

If you would like to contact Irene, write to her at:

Irene Dunlap
P.O. Box 10879
Costa Mesa, CA 92627

e-mail: irene@lifewriters.com

PERMISSIONS AND BIOGRAPHIES

"Out of the Churning Waters"

Reprinted by permission of Loretta Miller Mehl and Robert Mehl. ©2006 Loretta Miller Mehl

Loretta Miller Mehl crafts stories about her life as a farmer's daughter in the rural South. She also writes about the people she loves: her husband, four children, 13 gifted grandchildren, and friends. Her work appears in inspirational anthologies and devotional publications. Former secretary for the City of San Marino, California, she lived in that state for more than 40 years and now resides in Eugene, Oregon.

"Second Chance"

Reprinted by permission of Aisha K. Moore, Esq. ©2006 Aisha K. Moore, Esq.

Aisha K. Moore, Esq., is a wife and mother of five children. A graduate of Georgetown University Law Center, she's a licensed attorney specializing in intellectual property and employment discrimination law. She's living proof that

by the grace of God your past doesn't define your future and your beginning doesn't limit your end. She aspires to continue writing Christian fiction and nonfiction for young adults.

"The Brake of a Lifetime"

Reprinted by permission of Bruce Salvati. ©2006 Bruce Salvati

Bruce Salvati is a pastor and worship leader in Southern California. He and his wife, Lesley, serve God together by leading worship at a local church and teaching a variety of music lessons. They're blessed with five beautiful children.

"In His Hands"

Reprinted by permission of Phillip LaRue. ©2006 Phillip LaRue

Phillip LaRue is an accomplished artist who's released three CDs with Reunion Records. He's also a writer and producer for such projects as *The Message: Psalms* album with artists like Chris Rice, Ginny Owens, and Building 429. Throughout Phillip's life and career he's had a passion to help others see God's character. His desire for the future is to be real and vulnerable, no matter which door God leads him through. For more updated information about Phillip go to www.philliplarue.com.

"A Journey of Love"

Reprinted by permission of Linda Flock. ©2006 Linda Flock

Linda Flock is a successful insurance broker in Briarcliff Manor, New York. Most of her free time is consumed by her creative writing. She's pursuing photography, an avenue that gives her the opportunity to take her writing to another level. From greeting cards to short stories her words speak from her heart. Inspired by her own experience of healing, she continues to be driven by the power of prayer and the strength of her faith. She discovered her true passion while on a journey of love. You can e-mail her at sabinalf@yahoo.com.

"Near the Edge"

Reprinted by permission of Sirena Van Schaik. ©2006 Sirena Van Schaik

Sirena Van Schaik is an early childhood educator who's currently taking a few years' hiatus to pursue her dream of being a published writer. She enjoys reading, writing, scrapbooking, and just spending time with her husband, two children, and two Labrador retrievers. Sirena aspires to publish her first novel and is busy working on other articles for various magazines.

"The Plain Fact"

Reprinted by permission of Jacquelyn Abruzzini. ©2006 Jacquelyn Abruzzini

Jackie Abruzzini is an aspiring writer and artist who was born and raised in Petaluma, California. She now resides

in Arizona with her husband and hopes to have children someday. She utilizes her past experiences to teach a class for troubled and depressed women at her church.

"The New Girl"

Reprinted by permission of Tiffany O'Neill. ©2006 Tiffany O'Neill

Tiffany O'Neill is a homemaker and aspiring writer of fiction books for children and teens. She lives in San Francisco with her husband and two children.

"Thank You, Fozzie"

Reprinted by permission of Rusty Fischer. ©2001 Rusty Fischer

Rusty Fischer is the author of hundreds of poems, stories, essays, articles, and ideas for children. His poetry has appeared in such nationally recognized periodicals as *Boys' Quest* and *THE MAILBOX*, and his kids' stories have appeared in such best-selling anthologies as *Chicken Soup for the Preteen Soul*. His series of writing books for middle school students, *Creative Writing Made Easy*, continues to be a bestseller for Frank Schaffer Publications. His book from the *Wild, Wild West* series for popular library publisher Chelsea House Books, *Weapons of the Wild West*, brought such legendary heroes as Buffalo Bill and places such as the OK Corral to life in a way that pleased thousands of young readers.

"Stranded"

Reprinted by permission of Jenna King. ©2006 Jenna King

Jenna King is a University of Akron graduate with a bachelor of arts degree in communications. Jenna is an elementary school art teacher and writes children's books. Most of Jenna's stories are written about horses, animals, nature, drawing, painting, and art history, which are also her hobbies.

"Carried by the Good Shepherd"

Reprinted by permission of Katherine Knickerbocker. ©2006 Katherine Knickerbocker

Katherine Knickerbocker is currently a stay-at-home writer. She enjoys reading, writing, drawing, and working with people. She's planning on going to school to study for a career in health care. Katherine also wants to have a family of her own someday.

"A Flicker of Hope" and "The Voice Inside"

Reprinted by permission of Rachel Giffin. ©2006 Rachel Giffin

Rachel Giffin attends Moody Graduate School and is pursuing a master's in spiritual formation and discipleship. She has a bachelor of arts degree in educational ministries with a minor in psychology and aspires to write Christian curriculum and young adult Bible study materials. She enjoys traveling, reading, writing, and socializing with friends.

"Different"

Reprinted by permission of Ace Armstrong. ©2006 Ace Armstrong

Ace Armstrong currently resides in the city of Atascadero, a small town on the central coast of California. His interests include photography, and graphic and Web design. He enjoys listening to music, going to concerts, road trips, and traveling. Ace desires to travel the world and tell people about how the love of Christ has changed his life for the better.

"Back on the Right Track"

Reprinted by permission of Kristin Greene. ©2006 Kristin Greene

Kristin Greene is a junior in high school and a straight-A student who loves reading and writing. She's active in her church youth group and volunteer work within her community and enjoys spending her free time with friends. Kristin still lives with her grandparents and her mother. God has seen fit to give her a few more years with her mom, something she thanks him for every day.

"Never Alone"

Reprinted by permission of Laura Farrar. ©2006 Laura Farrar

Laura Farrar is a teen writer from California. These days she uses her life experience with shyness and depression to help other teens. She can be contacted by e-mail at LFwrites@yahoo.com and through her Web site: www. freewebs.com/laurafarrar.

"The Crash"

Reprinted by permission of Pamela Reilly. ©2006 Pamela Reilly

Pamela Reilly, former missionary and publisher, writes vocationally and in her spare time. She's married to the world's greatest husband and has four fantastic kids. In her "free" time Pamela enjoys discipling women and leading Bible studies, riding her motorcycle (as the driver, not the passenger), and making handmade soap. She's available to speak motivationally or share biblical insights with youth and women's groups. She may be reached at pamela@ephesians210.org.

"Reclaimed"

Reprinted by permission of Eric Hixon. ©2006 Eric Hixon

Eric Hixon lives in Alabama with his wife, Rebekah, and has five children: Hannah, Benjamin, Joshua, Mary Grace, and Faith. In 2007 they'll finalize the adoption of two children from Nicaragua. Eric is the founder and director of M.U.D. Ministries ("Making U Disciples"). He's also a sought-after Christian speaker for churches, youth groups, and men's conferences. Eric also has an international ministry in Nicaragua where he supports the physical and spiritual needs of many orphans. He's part of a national outdoor TV series as well. Eric can be contacted at www.mudministries.com, eric@mudministries.com, or 256-431-4429.

PERMISSIONS AND BIOGRAPHIES

"Satisfied"

Reprinted by permission of Paul Mishoe. ©2006 Paul Mishoe

Paul Mishoe is a senior at California State University, Bakersfield (CSUB) majoring in business administration with a concentration in management information systems. He works at CSUB part-time as an information technology assistant. He's involved in Campus Crusade for Christ and is treasurer for the student organizations and clubs council. His interests are in helping and encouraging others who are struggling in the same areas he did and witnessing to the lost. Paul can be contacted at Paulives4CHRIST@yahoo.com or www.myspace.com/Paulives4CHRIST.

"My Continuous Battle"

Reprinted by permission of Sarah Packard. ©2006 Sarah Packard

Sarah Packard currently works in a product distribution center in Minnesota. She plans on attending the University of Minnesota and studying music education. She enjoys reading, writing music, going to church, and spending time with her friends and family. Sarah aspires to be both a classical music performer and teacher and wants to someday settle down and have a family.

"Stitches, Scars, and Survival"

Reprinted by permission of Sarah Porter. ©2006 Sarah Porter

Sarah Porter is a graduate of Utah State University where she studied Family Consumer Human Development,

Public Relations, and English. She is now an employee of America First Credit Union and also owns a wedding video company. Sarah loves design, literature, and playing with her nieces and nephew. Sarah also loves learning and plans on continuing her education to become a counselor.

"All the Broken Pieces"

Reprinted by permission of Louise Russell. ©2006 Louise Russell

Louise Russell attends a Bible college in Sydney, Australia, where she plans to finish her bachelor of arts in ministry next year. She loves her friends, family, and dedicated boyfriend. Louise has big dreams to help her community and the young people of this generation. Upon graduation she wants to help teenagers like she once was, hopefully as youth pastor at a church. Most of all, she hopes to lead the lost to Jesus Christ, their only true hope.

"Piece by Piece"

Reprinted by permission of Katie Skarvinko and Barbara Skarvinko. ©2006 Katie Skarvinko

Katie Skarvinko loves doing what most teenage girls love to do: shop, hang out with friends, and just be her crazy self. She loves God more than anything and will do anything she can to live a respectable Christian life. She feels blessed to have loving parents who've done all they could to help her grow spiritually. If there's one verse in the Bible Katie lives by, it's "Trust in the Lord with all thine heart; and lean not unto thine own understanding" (Proverbs 3:5, KJV).

"Sinking Sand"

Reprinted by permission of Nancy C. Anderson. ©2006 Nancy C. Anderson

Nancy C. Anderson (www.nancycanderson.com) is a former teen from Minnesota who now lives in Orange County, California. She's an award-winning author and popular speaker who loves to encourage others to replace their fears with faith. Nancy has been featured on national media, including *The Montel Williams Show*, *The 700 Club*, and *FamilyLife Today*. Contact her at NancyCAnderson@ msn.com.

"Closer to the Fire"

Reprinted by permission of Madeline Shomos. ©2006 Madeline Shomos

Madeline Shomos tries to live every day for Christ. Nothing else is important. The rest is just extra.

"Sufficient for Me"

Reprinted by permission of Amanda Reese. ©2006 Amanda Reese

Amanda Reese attends Greenville College in Greenville, Illinois, and is studying English and religion. She's involved in tennis, soccer, and class council. Amanda enjoys reading, running, and spending time with her family and friends.

"Living Fortress"

Reprinted by permission of Brandon Tamblin. ©2006 Brandon Tamblin

Brandon Tamblin is a graphic designer for a budding multimedia company he owns with his best friend. He enjoys photography, writing poetry, playing indoor and outdoor soccer, mountain biking near his home, and snowboarding in the winter. He's recently engaged and preparing for a family of his own. Brandon enjoys working with young adults through discipleship and community teen programs. He hopes he can help young adults work through their family, social, spiritual, and mental health issues so they might attain success and find their unique identity in Christ.

"Swimming the Walk"

Reprinted by permission of Samuel R. Stephens. ©2006 Samuel R. Stephens

Samuel R. Stephens is currently enrolled in his third year at Oral Roberts University in Tulsa, Oklahoma, where he's pursuing a bachelor's degree in literary writing with a minor in journalism. He grew up in Maine where he enjoys spending his free time with friends and family in God's creation.

"Amazing Love"

Reprinted by permission of Laurie Vines. ©2006 Laurie Vines

Laurie Vines currently lives in Richmond, Virginia, with her husband and their two small children. She teaches public

speaking at John Tyler Community College and Spanish at Virginia Commonwealth University. Laurie enjoys movies, travel, adventure, and the company of loved ones. Her desire is to serve God through family, education, and the arts.

"Pointless Prayer"

Reprinted by permission of J. M. Butler. ©2006 J. M. Butler

J. M. Butler attends Indiana Wesleyan University in Marion, Indiana, and is pursuing a double major in pre-law and writing. In her free time she loves knitting, writing, hanging out with friends, and coming up with new things to do. Her hope is to write a best-selling series, get married, and have a family. If you would like to find out more, you can view her Web site at www.jmbutler.net.

"The Prom Date"

Reprinted by permission of Diana L. James. ©2006 Diana L. James

Diana L. James is an author, speaker, and former radio and television interview host in Idaho and California. Her articles and stories have appeared in numerous national magazines and in more than 20 books of collected short stories, including the *Chicken Soup for the Soul* books. Diana is also the author and compiler of the inspirational *Bounce Back* book series published by Horizon Books. She was cofounder and first president of a large writers' group in Idaho and has worked for several years on the teaching staff of CLASS, a national organization for training writers and speakers. Diana is currently teaching adult classes on

memoir-writing in the Boise area where she resides with her editor-husband, Max.

"In the Current"

Reprinted by permission of Joshua Nordgren. ©2006 Joshua Nordgren

Josh Nordgren is a loving husband, a songwriter and artist, and a high school youth pastor at Ventura Missionary Church. He enjoys surfing, skateboarding, and music. Check out www.myspace.com/acousticdiary to learn more.

"Redirected"

Reprinted by permission of Nicole Pipke. ©2006 Nicole Pipke

Nicole Pipke attends Concordia University College of Alberta and is majoring in child psychology. She enjoys horseback riding and spending time with her new puppy. Nicole aspires to become a chartered child psychologist and to provide psychology on a mission basis to those who wouldn't otherwise be able to afford it.

"Clearing the Way"

Reprinted by permission of Haley Vile. ©2006 Haley Vile

Haley currently lives in San Clemente, California. After completing her teaching credential, she moved to Malawi, Africa, to teach third grade at an international elementary school. Since returning home, she's been spending valuable time catching up with friends and family and waiting on

PERMISSIONS AND BIOGRAPHIES

God for the next adventure his plan entails. Haley can be reached via e-mail at haleyvile@gmail.com.

"A Snapshot Divinely Composed"

Reprinted by permission of Kellyn Walker. ©2006 Kellyn Walker

Kellyn Walker attends college at Taylor University and is currently studying photography and graphic design with a minor in French. She's involved at Taylor as the media and marketing services cabinet's digital photographer and enjoys art, reading, great music, and coffee. Kellyn aspires to use her love for people, art, and cosmetology in a way that brings much honor and glory to God.

"Hope in the Mourning"

Reprinted by permission of Alicia Aukerman. ©2006 Alicia Aukerman

Alie Aukerman attends Colorado Christian University and is majoring in psychology. She's involved in different student leadership positions on campus, including peer counseling and chapel assistant. She loves spending time outside and is involved in her church. She loves her family and friends. She aspires to be a light for Christ to hurting young people as a counselor for at-risk youth.

"Love That Heals"

Reprinted by permission of Elsa Kok Colopy. ©2006 Elsa Kok Colopy

Elsa Kok Colopy is former associate editor of *Focus on the Family* magazine and editor of the single-parent family edition. She is the author of four books: *A Woman Who Hurts, a God Who Heals*; *A Woman with a Past, a God with a Future*; *Settling for Less Than God's Best: A Relationship Check-up for Single Women*; and *The Single Mom's Guide to Finding Joy in the Chaos*, written for MOPS (Mothers of Preschoolers) to equip single mothers of preschoolers. A single mom for 12 years, Elsa has a heart for single parents. She also travels around the country leading retreats and conferences for a variety of audiences and currently works as a freelance writer and speaker based out of Bella Vista, Arkansas. Together she and her husband, Brian, have four children.

To learn more about Elsa, visit her Web site at www.elsakokcolopy.com.

"Letting Go"

Reprinted by permission of Kristina Marie Drummond. ©2006 Kristina Marie Drummond

Kristina Marie Drummond attends Westmont College and is majoring in liberal studies. She enjoys writing, beach volleyball, and spending time with friends and family. After college she aspires to be an elementary school teacher and has always dreamed of becoming a published author.

"Look How They Shine"

Reprinted by permission of Marleigh Dunlap. ©2006 Marleigh Dunlap

Marleigh Dunlap enjoys showing others the amazing love that's been so graciously shown to her, smiling, seeing and visiting as much of God's creation as she can, dreaming, seeing beyond the facades of culture, singing, and doing her best to make a difference in the lives of others. She hopes to serve people the rest of her life in whatever way God calls her to and desires always to be open to that call.

"Minute by Minute"

Reprinted by permission of Ryan Fischer. ©2006 Ryan Fischer

Ryan Fischer works for a homebuilder in Southern California as a superintendent. He's married and has one daughter. He enjoys spending time with his family, racing motocross, and offshore fishing in the Pacific Ocean.

"Enduring the Unendurable"

Reprinted by permission of Kristen McNulty. ©2006 Kristen McNulty

Kristen McNulty is a university student from Timmins, Ontario, Canada. She is the host of the syndicated *The Making A Difference (MAD) Christian Radio Show* (www. madradioshow.net). She enjoys reading, writing, and spending time in the outdoors with family and friends. Kristen has just published her first book, *Walking Through a Fallen World*. To find out more about it, go to www. kristenmcnulty.com

"On the Trail"

Reprinted by permission of Tom Beigle. ©2006 Tom Beigle

Tom Beigle travels and works odd jobs and aspires to be a writer, minister, and world-changer but none of those things in any currently existing sense. He's considered many directions for this life; however, the ambiguity of a life of adventure in the constant pursuit of Jesus (as if on some sort of spiritual treasure hunt) is currently the most appealing. He loves the unpredictability of each day and learning others' stories while enriching his own.

"Still Connected"

Reprinted by permission of Susan Rae Burns. ©2006 Susan Rae Burns

Susan Rae Burns is a retired academic advisor from the University of Missouri-Columbia. She's involved in mission work in her church, her state, and overseas. She and her husband are Christian clowns, and she enjoys writing the skits for their clown ministry as well as dramas for use at church. She lives in the home built by her great-grandparents, and her children are the sixth generation to live in this home.

"Streams of Mercy"

Reprinted by permission of Joseph Laughon. ©2006 Joseph Laughon

Joe Laughon, a junior in high school, lives in Ventura, California, and attends church at Ventura Missionary Church. He enjoys tangling with theological and political

issues, as well as comedians and funny movies. He plans to eventually serve God in the United States military. To contact Joe, write to him at laughonfamily@scbglobal. net.

"God Comes to History"

Reprinted by permission of Casey J. Day. ©2006 Casey J. Day

Casey Day feels someday she'll be a youth leader and hopes to start a church and bring a revolution to this generation. She's currently involved in Battle Cry Coalition. Casey loves her life and is very involved with her family, friends, and animals, and hopes one day to have a family and settle down.

"Playing by the Rules"

Reprinted by permission of Sandra Holmes McGarrity. ©2006 Sandra Holmes McGarrity

Sandra Holmes McGarrity is the author of three historical novels. Her writing has appeared in various magazines and books. Visit her Web page at http://hometown.aol. com/mygr8m8/myhomepage/books.html.

"The Richer Ones"

Reprinted by permission of Jessica Dunagan. ©2006 Jessica Dunagan

Jessica Dunagan recently graduated from Oklahoma Christian University, where she was an English writing major. She was involved in band and several campus literary venues. She enjoys reading, writing, and spending time with her family and husband. Jessica currently works as a technical editor but plans to pursue a master of fine arts degree in creative writing soon.

"What a Ride"

Reprinted by permission of Alistair Merryman. ©2006 Alistair Merryman

Alistair Merryman is currently working and living in Northern California. His passion for serving God and evangelizing to the lost has taken many shapes, from reaching out to strangers on street corners to creating an atmosphere for worship and Bible studies in coffeehouses. An accomplished jazz musician, Alistair now uses his musical talent to worship God. If you'd like to reach him, e-mail him at almerryman@gmail.com or to find out more about him, visit his Web site at www.digitalparable.com.

EVEN IN THE DARKEST HOUR, GOD KEEPS SHINING HIS LIGHT INTO OUR LIVES. *TRUE: VOL. 1* IS A COLLECTION OF STORIES FROM STUDENTS, ROCK STARS, AND OTHERS ABOUT WHAT HAPPENS WHEN GOD STEPS INTO THE MESS OF LIFE. IF YOU KNOW A STUDENT IN DOUBT, PAIN, OR STRUGGLE, GRAB THIS BOOK AND HELP THEM DISCOVER WHAT'S TRUE.

True Vol. 1
Real Stories About God Showing Up in the Lives of Teens
Irene Dunlap

RETAIL $12.99
ISBN 0-310-25268-7

Visit www.invertbooks.com or your local Christian bookstore.